CULTURE CONNECTION

For Improving
Language Skills and
Cultural Awareness

TAPESTRY

The **Tapestry** program of language materials is based on the concepts presented in *The Tapestry of Language Learning: The Individual in the Communicative Classroom* by Robin C. Scarcella & Rebecca L. Oxford.

Each title in this program focuses on:

Individual learner strategies and instruction

The relatedness of skills

Ongoing self-assessment

Authentic material as input

Theme-based learning linked to task-based instruction

Attention to all aspects of communicative competence

CULTURE CONNECTION

For Improving Language Skills and Cultural Awareness

Brenda Wegmann

Miki Knezevic

Patty Werner

Heinle & Heinle Publishers
A Division of Wadsworth, Inc.
Boston, Massachusetts, 02116, USA

The publication of *Culture Connection* was directed by the members of the Heinle & Heinle ESL Publishing Team:

David C. Lee, Editorial Director
John McHugh, Market Development Director
Lisa McLaughlin, Production Editor

Also participating in the publication of this program were:

Publisher: Stanley J. Galek
Editorial Production Manager: Elizabeth Holthaus
Assistant Editor: Kenneth Mattsson
Manufacturing Coordinator: Mary Beth Lynch
Full Service Project Manager/Compositor: PC&F, Inc.
Interior Design: Maureen Lauran
Cover Design: Maureen Lauran

02733

Manufactured in the United States of America.

ISBN: 0-8384-4121-1

Heinle & Heinle Publishers is a division of Wadsworth, Inc.

10 9 8 7 6 5 4 3 2 1

*To those in our families who
left their native lands and,
with courage and determination,
accepted the challenges of
a new culture*

PHOTO CREDITS

1, Michael Newman/PhotoEdit; 4, left, Robert Clay; 4, top, Todd Korol/First Light; 4, bottom, Michael Dwyer/Stock Boston; 14, Aaron Raphael/FPG; 14, Spencer Grant/Stock Boston; 21, Frank Siteman/Stock Boston; 28, top, Robert Clay; 28, bottom left, Jonathan Snow/The Image Works; 28, bottom right, Lorraine Rorke/The Image Works; 42, Michael Newman/PhotoEdit; 43, Jean-Claude Lejeune/Stock Boston; 49, Stephen McBrady/PhotoEdit; 63, Michael Dwyer/Stock Boston; 72, top left and right, Robert Clay; 72, bottom left, Margot Granitsas/The Image Works; 72, bottom right, Nicholas Sapieka/Stock Boston; 85, Robert Clay; 91, Rhoda Sidney/PhotoEdit; 97, Luc Novovitch/Gamma Liaison; 102, Topham/The Image Works; 108, Peter Menzel/Stock Boston; 111, Dick Luria/FPG; 111, bottom left, Peter Menzel/Stock Boston; 111, bottom right, D & I MacDonald/Photo Edit; 112, Dave Reede/First Light; 112, Robert Clay; 115, Richard Hutchings/PhotoEdit; 117, top left, Hemsey/Gamma Liaison; 117, top right, Maynard/Gamma Liaison; 117, bottom left, Glen Korengold/Stock Boston; 117, bottom right, Gale Zucker/Stock Boston; 122, Mark Antman/The Image Works; 137, Shmuel Thaler/Jeroboam; 141, Peter Menzel/Stock Boston; 146, David R. Austen/Stock Boston; 148, Rob Lang/FPG; 149, left, David Young-Wolff/PhotoEdit; 149, right, Owen Franklin/Stock Boston; 153, left, Kim Campbell/Gamma Liaison; 153, right, Mark Reinstein/FPG; 153, bottom, Cynthia Johnson/Gamma Liaison; 157, Elizabeth Hamlin/Stock Boston

ACKNOWLEDGMENTS

Cartoons

2, CALVIN AND HOBBES © 1992 Watterson. Reprinted with permission of UNIVERSAL PRESS SYNDICATE. All rights reserved.

30, 75, 125, From A MYSTERY WRAPPED IN AN ENIGMA SERVED ON A BED OF LETTUCE. Copyright © 1990 Mick Stevens. Reprinted by permission.

44, ZIGGY © 1992 ZIGGY AND FRIENDS INC. Distributed by UNIVERSAL PRESS SYNDICATE. Reprinted with permission.

118, From BOUND & GAGGED, UNCHAINED by Dana Summers. Reprinted by permission of Tribune Media Services.

156, CALVIN AND HOBBES © 1991 Watterson. Reprinted with permission of UNIVERSAL PRESS SYNDICATE. All rights reserved.

Text

11, "Cultural Differences Can Trip Up Witnesses" Edmonton Journal, 6 May 1993, page A3. Reprinted by permission of Southam News.

18-19, From THE BIG BOOK OF OPTICAL ILLUSIONS by Gyles Brandeth. Reprinted by permission of the author.

31, From THE DO'S AND TABOOS OF BODY LANGUAGE AROUND THE WORLD by Roger Axtell. Reprinted by permission of John Wiley & Sons, Inc.

37, From LIVING IN THE U.S.A. by Alison R. Lanier. Copyright © 1973 by Alison R. Lanier, Scribners. Copyright © 1978, 1981, 1988 by Alison R. Lanier. Reprinted by permission of the author.

48, From BABY NAME COUNTDOWN by Janet Schwegel. Reprinted by permission of Paragon House Publishers.

57, From NAMING OURSELVES, NAMING OUR CHILDREN: RESOLVING THE LAST NAME DILEMMA by Sharan Lebell. Reprinted by permission of the author.

60, "I'm Nobody, Who Are You?" by Emily Dickinson. Reprinted by permission of the publishers and the Trustees of Amherst College from THE POEMS OF EMILY DICKINSON. Thomas H. Johnson, ed., Cambridge, Mass: The Belknap Press of Harvard University Press. Copyright © 1951, 1955, 1979, 1983 by the President and Fellows of Harvard College.

70, From "How to Cook Like an American" by Laurie Colwin in GOURMET, April 1993. Copyright © 1993 by Laurie Colwin. Reprinted by permission of Donadio & Ashworth, Inc.

79, "A Most Embarrassing Moment" by Soon Hee Park. Reprinted by permission of the author.

86, From "Romancing the Bean" by Mark Ballering, Steep & Brew, Madison, Wisconsin. Reprinted by permission.

102, From ABOUT MARTIN LUTHER KING DAY by Mary Virginia Fox. Reprinted by permission of Enslow Publishers, Inc.

108, From GOOD NEIGHBORS: COMMUNICATING WITH THE MEXICANS by John C. Condon. Reprinted by permission of Intercultural Press, Inc.

121, Adapted from MEDICINE AND CULTURE: VARIETIES OF TREATMENT IN THE UNITED STATES, ENGLAND, WEST GERMANY AND FRANCE by Lynn Payer. Copyright © 1988 by Lynn Payer. Reprinted by permission of Henry Holt and Company, Inc. and Artellus Ltd.

129, From "Health: Take Charge! Questions You Should Ask" by Earl Ubell in PARADE MAGAZINE, April 26, 1992. Copyright © 1992 PARADE Publications, Inc. Reprinted by permission of the author.

131, Reprinted with permission © American Demographics.

145, From THAILAND: THE LAND OF SMILES by David C. Cooke. Copyright © 1971 and renewed 1992 by David C. Cooke. Reprinted by permission of the author.

155, From "Men Claim Desire to Become Less Macho" by Alan L. Otten in WALL STREET JOURNAL, March 31, 1992. Reprinted by permission of Wall Street Journal, © 1992 Dow Jones & Company, Inc. All Rights Reserved Worldwide.

161, "Marriage Is a Private Affair" from GIRLS AT WAR AND OTHER STORIES by Chinua Achebe. Reprinted by permission of the author.

WELCOME TO TAPESTRY

*E*nter the world of Tapestry! Language learning can be seen as an ever-developing tapestry woven with many threads and colors. The elements of the tapestry are related to different language skills like listening and speaking, reading and writing; the characteristics of the teachers; the desires, needs, and backgrounds of the students; and the general second language development process. When all these elements are working together harmoniously, the result is a colorful, continuously growing tapestry of language competence of which the student and the teacher can be proud.

This volume is part of the Tapestry program for students of English as a second language (ESL) at levels from beginning to "bridge" (which follows the advanced level and prepares students to enter regular postsecondary programs along with native English speakers). Tapestry levels include:

Beginning
Low Intermediate
High Intermediate
Low Advanced
High Advanced
Bridge

Because the Tapestry Program provides a unified theoretical and pedagogical foundation for all its components, you can optimally use all the Tapestry student books in a coordinated fashion as an entire curriculum of materials. (They will be published from 1993 to 1995 with further editions likely thereafter.) Alternatively, you can decide to use just certain Tapestry volumes, depending on your specific needs.

Tapestry is primarily designed for ESL students at postsecondary institutions in North America. Some want to learn ESL for academic or career advancement, others for social and personal reasons. Tapestry builds directly on all these motivations. Tapestry stimulates learners to do their best. It enables learners to use English naturally and to develop fluency as well as accuracy.

Tapestry Principles

The following principles underlie the instruction provided in all of the components of the Tapestry program.

EMPOWERING LEARNERS

Language learners in Tapestry classrooms are active and increasingly responsible for developing their English language skills and related cultural abilities. This self direction leads to better, more rapid learning. Some cultures virtually train their students to be passive in the classroom, but Tapestry weans them from passivity by providing exceptionally high interest materials, colorful and motivating activities, personalized self-reflection tasks, peer tutoring and other forms of cooperative learning, and powerful learning strategies to boost self direction in learning.

The empowerment of learners creates refreshing new roles for teachers, too. The teacher serves as facilitator, co-communicator, diagnostician, guide, and helper. Teachers are set free to be more creative at the same time their students become more autonomous learners.

HELPING STUDENTS IMPROVE THEIR LEARNING STRATEGIES

Learning strategies are the behaviors or steps an individual uses to enhance his or her learning. Examples are taking notes, practicing, finding a conversation partner, analyzing words, using background knowledge, and controlling anxiety. Hundreds of such strategies have been identified. Successful language learners use language learning strategies that are most effective for them given their particular learning style, and they put them together smoothly to fit the needs of a given language task. On the other hand, the learning strategies of less successful learners are a desperate grab-bag of ill-matched techniques.

All learners need to know a wide range of learning strategies. All learners need systematic practice in choosing and applying strategies that are relevant for various learning needs. Tapestry is one of the only ESL programs that overtly weaves a comprehensive set of learning strategies into language activities in all its volumes. These learning strategies are arranged in six broad categories throughout the Tapestry books:

Forming concepts
Personalizing
Remembering new material
Managing your learning
Understanding and using emotions
Overcoming limitations

The most useful strategies are sometimes repeated and flagged with a note, "It Works! Learning Strategy . . ." to remind students to use a learning strategy they have already encountered. This recycling reinforces the value of learning strategies and provides greater practice.

RECOGNIZING AND HANDLING LEARNING STYLES EFFECTIVELY

Learners have different learning styles (for instance, visual, auditory, hands-on; reflective, impulsive; analytic, global; extroverted, introverted; closure-oriented, open). Particularly in an ESL setting, where students come from vastly different cultural backgrounds, learning style differences abound and can cause "style conflicts."

Unlike most language instruction materials, Tapestry provides exciting activities specifically tailored to the needs of students with a large range of learning styles. You can use any Tapestry volume with the confidence that the activities and materials are intentionally geared for many different styles. Insights from the latest educational and psychological research undergird this style-nourishing variety.

OFFERING AUTHENTIC, MEANINGFUL COMMUNICATION

Students need to encounter language that provides authentic, meaningful communication. They must be involved in real-life communication tasks that cause them to *want* and *need* to read, write, speak, and listen to English. Moreover, the tasks—to be most effective—must be arranged around themes relevant to learners.

Themes like family relationships, survival in the educational system, personal health, friendships in a new country, political changes, and protection of the environment are all valuable to ESL learners. Tapestry focuses on topics like these. In every Tapestry volume, you will see specific content drawn from very broad areas such as home life, science and technology, business, humanities, social sciences, global issues, and multiculturalism. All the themes are real and important, and they are fashioned into language tasks that students enjoy.

At the advanced level, Tapestry also includes special books each focused on a single broad theme. For instance, there are two books on business English, two on English for science and technology, and two on academic communication and study skills.

UNDERSTANDING AND VALUING DIFFERENT CULTURES

Many ESL books and programs focus completely on the "new" culture, that is, the culture which the students are entering. The implicit message is that ESL students should just learn about this target culture, and there is no need to understand their own culture better or to find out about the cultures of their international classmates. To some ESL students, this makes them feel their own culture is not valued in the new country.

Tapestry is designed to provide a clear and understandable entry into North American culture. Nevertheless, the Tapestry Program values *all* the cultures found in the ESL classroom. Tapestry students have constant opportunities to become "culturally fluent" in North American culture while they are learning English, but they also have the chance to think about the cultures of their classmates and even understand their home culture from different perspectives.

INTEGRATING THE LANGUAGE SKILLS

Communication in a language is not restricted to one skill or another. ESL students are typically expected to learn (to a greater or lesser degree) all four language skills: reading, writing, speaking, and listening. They are also expected to develop strong grammatical competence, as well as become socioculturally sensitive and know what to do when they encounter a "language barrier."

Research shows that multi-skill learning is more effective than isolated-skill learning, because related activities in several skills provide reinforcement and refresh the learner's memory. Therefore, Tapestry integrates all the skills. A given

Tapestry volume might highlight one skill, such as reading, but all other skills are also included to support and strengthen overall language development.

However, many intensive ESL programs are divided into classes labeled according to one skill (Reading Comprehension Class) or at most two skills (Listening/Speaking Class or Oral Communication Class). The volumes in the Tapestry Program can easily be used to fit this traditional format, because each volume clearly identifies its highlighted or central skill(s).

Grammar is interwoven into all Tapestry volumes. However, there is also a separate reference book for students, *The Tapestry Grammar,* and a Grammar Strand composed of grammar "work-out" books at each of the levels in the Tapestry Program.

Other Features of the Tapestry Program

PILOT SITES

It is not enough to provide volumes full of appealing tasks and beautiful pictures. Users deserve to know that the materials have been pilot-tested. In many ESL series, pilot testing takes place at only a few sites or even just in the classroom of the author. In contrast, Heinle & Heinle Publishers have developed a network of Tapestry Pilot Test Sites throughout North America. At this time, there are approximately 40 such sites, although the number grows weekly. These sites try out the materials and provide suggestions for revisions. They are all actively engaged in making Tapestry the best program possible.

AN OVERALL GUIDEBOOK

To offer coherence to the entire Tapestry Program and especially to offer support for teachers who want to understand the principles and practice of Tapestry, we have written a book entitled, *The Tapestry of Language Learning. The Individual in the Communicative Classroom* (Scarcella and Oxford, published in 1992 by Heinle & Heinle).

A Last Word

We are pleased to welcome you to Tapestry! We use the Tapestry principles every day, and we hope these principles—and all the books in the Tapestry Program—provide you the same strength, confidence, and joy that they give us. We look forward to comments from both teachers and students who use any part of the Tapestry Program.

Rebecca L. Oxford
University of Alabama
Tuscaloosa, Alabama

Robin C. Scarcella
University of California at Irvine
Irvine, California

PREFACE

Culture Connection is a multi-skill text that focuses on the connection between language and culture. It has two primary objectives: to improve basic communication skills and to increase cultural awareness. As a textbook it may be used in low-intermediate classes streamed for Culture, Conversation, Speaking and Listening, Reading, or Communication Skills.

Culture Connection intertwines language skills and world view, encouraging strategies that facilitate effective communication. This can lead to increased confidence and a more pleasurable experience in the United States or Canada. Cultural similarities and differences around the world are explored to give students a basis for understanding North American cultures as well as for gaining a greater appreciation of their own heritage.

Opening Up, Opening Out

The text begins with relatively "safe" themes—aspects of culture that are readily noticed and discussed by almost any visitor—and easy, structured activities. It progresses slowly into deeper questions of culture and somewhat "riskier" activities that require introspection or interaction with others. Varied tasks challenge students to become aware of their cultural filters, to sharpen their powers of observation and analysis, to see situations from other points of view, and to explore new ways of communicating.

Culture Connection also presents an introduction to basic social skills and to some of the critical thinking modes and ways of interacting that are essential in North American academic and professional life: categorizing, comparing and contrasting, setting goals and priorities, expressing personal opinions, talking about emotions, agreeing and disagreeing, participating in open discussions and debates, and pair and group efforts in completing tasks, for example. Thus, at the same time that students are communicating about aspects of culture, they are doing so in ways that may be new to them.

Reasons For Using a Culture Text at an Early Level

Culture is a high-interest topic for ESL students. They are curious about North American customs and attitudes and enjoy learning about them. Learning about culture is also an aid to learning English. The language-culture connection is deeply embedded in virtually all linguistic and social aspects of communication. Students arrive with preprogrammed sets of structures, sound systems, customs and attitudes. Much of this is culturally determined and unconscious, yet it seems as natural as the sun in the sky. If students are encouraged to observe and examine cultural differences, and the similarities that underlie them, they can avoid making false assumptions about what they hear and read. They are then more likely to give correct messages, rather than forcing English words into preconceived patterns from their own culture.

FOR CULTURE CLASSES

Culture Connection presents materials and tasks designed to help students to move through the various stages of cultural awareness. It begins by encouraging students to see the importance of cultural influences through the development of the skills of observation, comparison, and contrast. The next step is the examination of varied points of view on many aspects of language and culture and the exchange of ideas and opinions about them. The aim at this stage is to enable students to evaluate the advantages and disadvantages of actions and attitudes, without immediately accepting or rejecting them as *good* or *bad*. Finally, a context is created for the integration of what has been learned, so that students may come to understand and appreciate ideas and customs from other cultures, and at the same time see and value themselves and their own heritage as an important part of a many-cultured world.

Built into this program of cultural awareness is a graded program of materials and tasks for the improvement of reading, writing, and conversational skills. Thus, the text looks at culture through a truly multi-skill approach to language.

FOR CONVERSATION OR SPEAKING/LISTENING CLASSES

Culture Connection can serve as either the primary text or a supplementary text for low-intermediate classes focusing on oral skills. The text engages students in a wide variety of speaking tasks, such as describing, comparing and contrasting, telling stories, asking for clarification, accepting and declining, categorizing, and expressing opinions. It also encourages observation of speech in natural settings, listening analysis, imitation of sounds, modeling, rhyming, and many interactive tasks, such as interviewing, conducting surveys, indulging in small talk, and role-playing. The progression is from short, easy and relatively structured interventions in early chapters to longer, more demanding and open-ended interactions in the later chapters. A major goal of the text is to enable students to develop their skills for expressing agreement and disagreement, and participating in group discussions.

FOR READING CLASSES

Culture Connection may be used as the primary text for a reading class that focuses on culture because the basic reading skills are presented: finding the main idea, scanning, skimming, guessing the meaning from context, understanding idioms, using the title and illustrations for anticipating, making predictions, previewing an extended reading, and so on. The readings are authentic selections written in a variety of styles and drawn from many sources: books, newspapers, magazines and textbooks; many are shortened and some have been slightly adapted. The writing and discussion assignments can be used selectively to augment the reading program.

Vocabulary acquisition, and the learning of vocabulary skills as an adjunct to reading skills, is presented and practiced throughout the text, with special emphasis on idioms, synonyms, antonyms, and word families.

In general, the reading selections are short and easy, especially those at the beginning, which deal with rather objective, impersonal subjects. Longer, more personal and thought-provoking selections are placed toward the end of the book. The last chapter presents, as an Extended Reading Challenge in original and unadapted form, an emotionally engaging story about the conflict between an individual and his family's traditions, written by the well-known Nigerian writer, Chinua Achebe. It is used to introduce students to strategies for longer readings and encourages them to continue with such reading after the course. The story is divided into four sections with aids for comprehension and discussion.

How to Use This Text

Chapter One is an introductory chapter and as such has a different format from the other six. It is meant to be worked through without prior preparation and to introduce the students to the general aims and procedures of the course. Chapters Two through Six each begin with a brief introduction to the chapter's theme and a listing of possible goals. These chapters end with a section called *Looking Back* that invites students to reflect upon what they have learned and how well they have accomplished the goals mentioned at the chapter's beginning. This is followed by some vocabulary review exercises, since vocabulary acquisition is a constant goal throughout all chapters.

All chapters are divided into four or five themes, some with two parts, labeled A and B. Typically, one or two themes can be presented in a class period. The text can be modified to fit shorter courses by dropping one or two themes from any given chapter. The only adjustment needed as a consequence might be to delete some words from the Vocabulary Review exercises at the end of that chapter. Alternatively, instructors may choose to take all themes and skip some of the exercises and activities

The Appendix on page 171 gives answers for certain exercises, when it is so stated in their directions.

THE TEACHER'S MANUAL

The Teacher's Manual for *Culture Connection* is available from the publisher; it provides a complete Answer Key for all exercises in the text which have specific answers. The Teacher's Manual also includes additional ideas and activities for every chapter along with a detailed explanation of how to teach a sample chapter.

MANAGING PAIR AND GROUP ACTIVITIES

Culture Connection includes numerous pair and group activities. These provide an excellent opportunity for more student involvement and the development of conversational skills. Here are some suggestions for implementing pair and group work.

Our classes are filled with students who have different styles of learning. Because of both cultural and individual differences, some students will have more difficulty than others in participating in pair work and group activities. For some, the challenge will be in learning how to speak up and express their opinions; for others, the challenge will be in learning to limit their own interventions and listen to the opinions of others.

The first few times that pair work is introduced, it is a good idea to present it in a very clear and structured way, following certain steps.

Suggested Steps for Pair Work

1. Assign a partner for each student. If there is an odd number, work with the extra student yourself or change one pair into a trio, telling them to take turns.
2. Once everyone has a partner, explain the assignment clearly to the whole class, and make sure everybody knows what to do. Stress the benefits of practicing English in a conversational manner with a partner. Remind them that *everyone* has an accent and even North Americans from different regions sometimes have trouble understanding each other. Tell them to say to their partner, "Could you repeat that, please?" when they do not understand. Then state clearly, "Begin now."
3. While students are working, walk around the class, showing a general interest in what is happening. If some pairs seem to be having difficulties or have lapsed into silence, offer a helpful suggestion. The first few pair tasks should not last more than a few minutes.
4. At a certain point, say, "Time's up. Let's find out what you have learned." Reconvene the class as a whole, and call on all or most students to say something about what they have done.

Don't be discouraged if students don't interact brilliantly at first. Sometimes it takes practice to learn to work in pairs, but it is well worth the effort. After students have had some experience, you can relax the procedure or vary it, occasionally letting them choose their own partner or extending the time limit when students seem very involved, and you won't always have to call on students afterwards for a report. With familiarity, pair work can function as a useful and flexible tool which you can call upon frequently to introduce variety into the classroom. Pair work can include interviews, simple questions and answers, problem-solving or role-playing.

The procedure for group tasks and group discussions is similar to the above section on pair work, but with a few additional steps.

Suggested Additional Steps for Group Work

1. After assigning groups and explaining the task clearly, you should assign a group leader to direct the other members. Explain that this person should have everyone tell his or her name and then call on everyone in turn to help with the task. Emphasize the importance of everyone participating. If the task is an open discussion, present students with your own guidelines or refer them to the next section.

2. Once again, be sure to walk around and appear interested in what is going on in the groups. Join different groups for a while, remaining a silent observer unless called upon. If one student is dominating too much or not participating at all, refer the whole group to the *Tips For Participating in Group Discussion* and ask them how well they think their group is following them. Group work will usually last longer than pair work. However, be sure to end the task before everyone finishes and interest starts to flag. It is not necessary that every group accomplish the whole task.

3. Afterwards, call on someone from the group other than the leader, perhaps a volunteer, to report to the class. Again, after your class has some experience with group work, you can make the procedure more relaxed and flexible.

An important goal of this text is to help students learn to participate more effectively in group discussions. The following section presents some tips regarding this.

Tips for Students on Participating in Group Discussions

Groups discussions are very common in North American life: in business, politics, science, the arts and even during social occasions. Therefore, it is very useful to learn how to participate in group discussions. How can you do this? Well, as an old proverb says, *Practice makes perfect.* Here are some guidelines. Read them through from time to time and try to follow them during class and small-group discussions.

1. Don't remain silent all the time. The basic North American belief in equality means that everyone has the right to state an opinion. Even if there are older people present, or people in higher positions, your participation is appreciated and expected. The general feeling is that if someone doesn't say anything, it's because he or she has nothing to say.

2. Don't dominate the discussion. Give your opinions, but don't talk too long. After a while, be quiet and give someone else a turn. This also relates to the North American belief in equality and fair play.

3. Don't let anyone else dominate. If someone keeps on talking and talking, without giving anyone a chance, say, "Excuse me, but let's hear some other opinions now."

4. If you don't understand something, ask about it. This is not seen as weakness, but as a sign of interest and involvement.

5. You do not have to be absolutely sure of your idea in order to offer it. You can say that you *think* or *feel* a certain way but are not sure about it. This is seen as an exploration of a topic and is not looked down upon. Who knows? Maybe your idea is not completely correct but it could lead to other good ideas from other member of the group.

6. If you can't think of any ideas to offer, ask a question about the topic. Asking questions is considered participation.

7. If you agree with someone, say so. Say, "I agree with your idea about . . ." Then give your reason for agreeing or add another idea.

8. If you don't agree with someone, say so. Say, "I don't completely agree with you about . . ." Then give your reason for not agreeing. North Americans consider disagreement healthy. It can lead to better understanding of ideas. Of course, you should be polite. (By adding the word *completely,* you are making your statement softer and more polite.)

PREFACE

9. Don't get "hot under the collar." Learn to disagree without becoming disagreeable. If you find yourself getting upset, take a deep breath and keep quiet for a while.

10. Listen. Open yourself to the ideas and opinions of others. Discussions can be a lot of fun and a wonderful way to learn about the world.

Acknowledgments

Through the many ups and downs of preparing this text, we have enjoyed and benefited from working with the *Tapestry* team at Heinle and Heinle. In particular, a big thank you to the following: Rebecca Oxford and Robin Scarcella for their inspiration and example in addition to the excellent editing and encouragement from Rebecca; David Lee, Editorial Director, and Ken Mattsson, Assistant Editor, for their fine, flexible direction and supervision of text development; to Tom Scovel for emphasizing to us the universalities that underlie cultural differences; and to Lisa McLaughlin of Heinle and Heinle, and Elaine Hall of PC&F Inc., for their excellent assistance during production.

At this time, we would like to express our heartfelt gratitude to Kim Brown of Portland State University, whose perceptive comments on cultural observation helped us to get on the right track at the beginning, and whose continuing, creative direction has served as a guiding light, without which this text would not exist in its present form.

Many others have contributed to the ideas which have shaped *Culture Connection*. Special thanks to Pamela Bona, Foreign Student Advisor, Office of International Students, the Pennsylvania State University, for the insights she shared during an unforgettable ride through the mountains of Argentina; to Dr. B.H. Cinnader for describing cultural nuances based on his experiences around the world; to Mrs. Pauline S. Dominski for providing materials for a reading selection; to Anné Knezevic for materials and helpful suggestions; to Yen Tang Nguyen, whose support and friendship have opened windows onto new cultural dimensions; and to the many international students at the University of Wisconsin, Madison, and especially Kye Sook Kim, who shared their adventures and misadventures in experiencing a new culture.

We also owe a great debt of gratitude to our husbands and children for their patience, support and long-suffering during the writing of this text.

Finally, we want to express our gratitude to the reviewers whose excellent suggestions proved helpful, and sometimes crucial, to the final form of this text. *Culture Connection* is very different from the book we had first envisaged two years ago, much better, we believe. This improvement is largely due to the evaluations and critiques made by the following reviewers:

Susan Bangs, Harrisburg Area Community College
Kim Brown, Portland State University
Sandra Carretin, University of Houston
Kathy Clark, Texas A&M University
Marta Dmytrenko-Ahrabian, Wayne State University
Rebecca Oxford, University of Alabama
Tom Scovel, San Francisco State University

CONTENTS

4 *Why Do Some Foods
Taste So Good?*   63

THEME 3: WHERE, WHEN, AND HOW WE EAT: SIMILARITIES AND DIFFERENCES

THEME 4: WORDS AND RITUALS INVOLVING FOODS

LOOKING BACK ON CHAPTER 4

5 *How, When, and Why Do We Celebrate?*   *91*

INTRODUCTION

THEME 1: HOLIDAYS AROUND THE WORLD

THEME 2: CELEBRATING THE BEGINNING OF A NEW YEAR

6 *What Are the Secrets of Good Health?* 115

THEME 4: THE INFLUENCE OF EMOTIONS ON HEALTH

LOOKING BACK ON CHAPTER 6

7 Why Are Friendship and Love So Important? *141*

INTRODUCTION

THEME 1: FRIENDSHIP MEANS DIFFERENT THINGS TO DIFFERENT PEOPLE

THEME 2: THE RITUALS OF SOCIALIZING AND DATING

THEME 3: CHANGING VALUES, CHANGING LANGUAGE

THEME 4: LOVE AND/OR MARRIAGE

An Introduction: Adjusting to a New Culture

A new culture generally means a new language. But it also means other new factors. Sometimes a person's customs and ways of thinking prepare him or her for the new situation. Sometimes they don't.

A. Two Descriptions

LEARNING STRATEGY

Forming Concepts: Reading without trying to understand each word helps you concentrate on the important ideas.

Imagine you have just arrived in a new culture. Read these two descriptions of that experience.

Description 1

Things seem very different and new. The buildings have unusual shapes. They are too big (or too small). The colors are different. Everything looks gray and brown. It's hard to know how to cross the street. Where is the downtown? There is a strange smell and some kind of burning from a factory. And the food! It has no taste at all. The air is cold and damp, unbelievably damp. The sidewalk feels different under my feet—bumpy, not smooth. Maybe that is why the people walk in a different way.

Description 2

Everything looks pretty much the same as in my culture. The buildings seem to be about the same height. The doors, windows, elevators, and escalators seem identical. The cars are the same makes. The buses, subways, and trains run in the same way. The colors, smells, and sounds are familiar. The air feels dry and warm just like at home. The people are all in a hurry, too, just like at home. Of course, the food tastes a little unusual, but it is not bad. Not much looks different on the surface.

Calvin and Hobbes   **Bill Watterson**

It's Like Landing on a New Planet

TASK 1: FINDING THE MAIN IDEA

1. What is the main idea of each description?
2. How are they different?
3. Which description is more like your own experience (or what you imagine) of coming to a new culture? Explain.

LEARNING STRATEGY

**Managing Your Learning: Rereading for details increases
your comprehension.**

TASK 2: MAKING A LIST OF SENSORY DETAILS

The two descriptions contain many small details (bits of information). We notice details through our five senses of sight, sound, smell, taste and touch (the feeling on our skin). How many details are mentioned for each of the senses in Description A? And in Description B? Make a chart like the one that follows. Find as many details as you can and write them in the correct places. Then compare your lists with those of your classmates, and answer the questions.

	DESCRIPTION 1	DESCRIPTION 2
Sight	_____	_____
Sound	_____	_____
Smell	_____	_____
Taste	_____	_____
Touch	_____	_____

1. In your opinion, which of the two descriptions is more true to life for most visitors to a new culture?
2. Do any details of Description A remind you of your own experience (or of what you imagine) in a new culture? If so, which ones?
3. Do any parts of Description B remind you of your own experience or of what you imagine? If so, which ones?
4. Look at the last line of Description B. What does it mean? What kind of differences are "on the surface"? What kind of differences can be "below the surface"?

B. A Visualization Exercise

Look at the three photos. Visualize yourself (see yourself in "your mind's eye") in the places shown in each one. Then follow the instructions below.

TASK 1: WRITING YOUR OWN DESCRIPTION

Choose one of the photos. Imagine that you have just arrived at the place in the photo. Think about what you would see, hear, smell, feel and taste. Write a description of it. What activities might be a problem there? Crossing the street? Understanding the signs? Finding a good restaurant? Tell which photo you are writing about (left, top, or bottom), then write a short description. Use one of these as your first sentence:

a. I have just arrived in this place, and everything seems different and strange to me.

b. I have just arrived in this place, and everything seems the same as at home.

c. I have just arrived in this place, and some things seem the same and other things seem unusual.

Your teacher may want to read your description. Or your teacher may ask for volunteers (people who offer to do something) to read their descriptions, or parts of them. Compare ideas with your classmates.

TASK 2: TALKING ABOUT A PICTURE

Bring a photo or picture of a place you like or don't like. Show it to the class and talk about it. Explain why you like it or don't like it.

LEARNING STRATEGY

Forming Concepts: Guessing intelligently, whether right or wrong, promotes your language learning.

TASK 3: GUESSING AND DRAWING (MAKING) CONCLUSIONS

Look back to page 4 and answer these questions.

1. Guess where the photos on page 4 were taken. Which do you think were taken in the United States or Canada?
2. Look up the answers in the Answer Appendix at the end of the book. Are you surprised by any of the answers?
3. Do you think the people living in the three different places speak English in the same way? Why or why not?
4. What details show you that North America is a *multicultural society* (a society made of many different cultures)?
5. Everybody in the world has an accent. True or false? Explain.

THEME 2: SETTING REASONABLE GOALS

A goal is an aim or objective, something you want to do. In this course you want to improve your basic English skills (speaking, listening, reading, and writing). You also want to learn about North American culture and culture in general. How much time do you have to do this? It is important to set reasonable goals. That means possible goals. (It is not reasonable to try for the impossible.)

Managing Your Learning: Setting goals for yourself helps you improve areas that are important to you.

TASK 1: TELLING THE DIFFERENCE BETWEEN REASONABLE AND UNREASONABLE GOALS

Look at the following list of goals. Check the ones you think are reasonable for you in this course. Explain why the others are not reasonable.

1. _____ Learn to talk like a native speaker of English.

2. _____ Acquire (get) 2,000 new English words in my active vocabulary.

3. _____ Learn to express some ideas in clear English sentences.

4. _____ Discover (find out) everything about North American culture so I won't make any mistakes.

5. _____ Improve my reading ability.

6. _____ Gain a working pronunciation (ability to say the sounds) of English so I can be understood.

7. _____ Acquire the ability to understand English speech, radio, movies, and TV.

8. _____ Learn what to do when I don't understand someone in English.

9. _____ Find out some practical information about U.S. and Canadian customs and attitudes.

10. _____ Acquire 200–300 new words to use in English, and learn to understand many more.

11. _____ Gain a better understanding of differences among cultures.

12. _____ Master the art of writing books in English.

13. _____ Learn how to have conversations with North Americans.

14. _____ Learn what to say and do in many social situations in North America.

TASK 2: MAKING A LIST OF PERSONAL GOALS

Answer the questions. Then choose the five goals from the list in Task 1 that you think are most important. Change the words if you want. Write down the goals in the order of importance, with number *one* as most important. Compare lists with your classmates.

1. Do you know what *active vocabulary* means? Can you guess the difference between a person's active vocabulary and his or her passive vocabulary? Which is bigger?
2. Which of the four basic skills is most important for success in school or university? For success in a job or profession?
3. Some people find reading easy in a new language, but have trouble speaking. For other people, it is the opposite. Some have the most trouble with understanding speech, or with writing. Which skill is hardest for you? Which one is easiest?
4. Some people acquire good skills in English but have problems in North America because they don't understand the culture. In your opinion, does this happen in other cultures too? Explain.

THEME 3: HOW TO ACQUIRE VOCABULARY

Vocabulary acquisition (the acquiring—getting—of new words) is an important goal for every person learning a new language. How many words do you think you know in your native language? How did you learn them? How do you plan to learn new words in English?

Many teachers suggest a personal vocabulary notebook as one of the best methods of acquiring vocabulary. A student buys a small notebook just for vocabulary. He or she carries it all the time and writes down new or important words every day. Why do you think this method works so well?

Threads

Webster's *Third International Dictionary* shows over 450,000 words in English.

A. Learning Vocabulary by Word Association

This book teaches vocabulary in several different ways. One way is by association (linking). Our human brains accept new words more easily by associating (linking, connecting) them to something else. So, learn new words along with their *synonyms* (words that mean the same thing) or definitions. Or learn new words with *antonyms* (words that mean exactly the opposite, like *in* and *out*). Or learn *word families,* variations of a root word, like *interest, interested, interesting.* Practice learning by association by doing the following exercises. They present vocabulary used up to now in this chapter. See if you have learned some new words today.

TASK 1: LEARNING VOCABULARY WITH SYNONYMS

Match each word in the first column to its synonym in the second column. Then say both. There is an extra word in the column on the right. Can you guess why?

1. _____ acquire   a. identical
2. _____ arrive   b. change
3. _____ association   c. find out
4. _____ discover   d. possible
5. _____ goal   e. get
6. _____ modify   f. unusual
7. _____ reasonable   g. detail
8. _____ same   h. come
9. _____ strange   i. linking
                                  j. aim

TASK 2: LEARNING VOCABULARY WITH DEFINITIONS

Match each word in the first column to its definition in the second column. Then say both.

1. _____ acquisition   a. referring to the five senses
2. _____ details   b. the act of getting or gaining something
3. _____ multicultural   c. imagine, see in "your mind's eye"
4. _____ sensory   d. someone who offers to do something
5. _____ visualize   e. pronounce very carefully
6. _____ volunteer   f. made up of many cultures
                           g. bits of information

TASK 3: LEARNING VOCABULARY WITH ANTONYMS

Match each word in the first column to its antonym in the second column. Then say both.

1. _____ damp   a. listen
2. _____ identical   b. cold
3. _____ leave   c. active
4. _____ old   d. dry
5. _____ passive   e. familiar
6. _____ smooth   f. imagine
7. _____ talk   g. new
8. _____ unusual   h. bumpy
9. _____ warm   i. different
                           j. arrive

TASK 4: GUESSING THE MYSTERY WORDS

Can this be English? Here are five mystery words with their letters scrambled (mixed–up). Unscramble the letters (or guess the words). Write them down. Remember: there are *five* of them. Answers are in the Answer Appendix at the end of the book.

1. chuto _____

2. thigs _____

3. setta _____

4. niraghe _____

5. lemls _____

B. Learning Idioms and Figures of Speech

When we explain the meaning of *visualize,* we say it means to see in "the mind's eye." This is really a *figure of speech.* The mind does not really have an eye. We use this figure, or picture, to help us understand. Common groups of words using figures of speech are called *idioms.* They often have meanings that are very different from what the words say. Look at the four idioms in the box. The pictures show what the words say. But the sentences show us the real meaning. Look at the pictures to help you visualize the idiom. Read the sentences to understand the meaning. Then answer the questions in Task 1 that follows.

Vocabulary Study: Four Idioms

1. brainstorm
Hey, don't worry about that problem because I just had a *brainstorm!* Let's *brainstorm* for a while and try to find the solution to our problem.

2. to learn by heart
We have to learn all the formulas *by heart* for tomorrow's test.

**3. to develop a
thick skin**
Their negative words
don't bother him now
because he has
developed a thick skin.

**4. to take the bull
by the horns**
She decided *to take
the bull by the horns*
and send out a job
application.

TASK 1: QUESTIONS

1. Which idiom means *to memorize* or *to learn something exactly?*
2. Which idiom means *to take direct action?*
3. Which of the idioms can be used as a noun or a verb?
4. Which idiom refers to making yourself strong in a difficult situation?
5. Think back to a time when you decided to take the bull by the horns. What did you do?
6. Sometimes managers in big companies decide to hold brainstorming sessions with their employees. In your opinion, why do they do this?

Forming Concepts: Understanding the main idea helps you comprehend the entire reading.

TASK 2: READING FOR THE MAIN IDEA

The following selection is from a Canadian newspaper. It gives an example from real life of the importance of idioms. Read only for the main idea. Do not stop because you cannot understand some words. Read to the end. If necessary, read the selection two or three times. Then finish the sentence about the main idea.

Cultural Differences Can Trip Up Witnesses

Ottawa

Here is a courtroom scene from a new video prepared for judges:

The Chinese witness seems confused by the questions from the white lawyer.

"Now Mr. Chan, when your tenant didn't pay the rent, was that the straw that broke the camel's back*? You were at the end of your rope, weren't you? Could we say that for three months you were burning the candle at both ends in order to earn more money?"

"Mr. Chan, we're waiting for your answer," said the lawyer.

"I don't understand what you're saying," said Mr. Chan, "about the . . . camel. You asked me about a camel."

Ed Lam of the Canadian Ethnocultural Council said the scene shows a common problem. "You can see it's important in a courtroom to speak to a witness from a non-dominant culture in clear language, without idioms."

—*Edmonton Journal*

IT WORKS! Learning Strategy: Guessing Helps Understanding.

The straw that broke the camel's back is an idiom that means *the last thing in a series of bad things that causes a bad result*. It comes from an old story about a man who puts many items on the back of a camel until finally he adds one piece of straw and the camel falls down dead. Two other idioms are used in this paragraph. *To be at the end of your rope* means to be very upset and desperate. *To be burning the candle at both ends* means to be doing so many activities that you get very tired.

Remembering New Material: Forming a picture in your mind makes it easier to remember idioms.

THE MAIN IDEA

This reading shows that idioms are important because:

_____

_____

_____

_____

_____

_____

_____

_____

_____

THEME 4: KEEPING A PERSONAL JOURNAL FOR FREEWRITING

Learning to write well, in English or in any language, takes regular practice. It is like learning a new sport. The more you practice, the better you become. For example, you don't learn a good tennis serve by playing only once a month. A good serve comes after many hours, weeks, or even months of practice.

Practicing *freewriting* in a journal can improve your writing skills. Freewriting means writing passages on a regular basis, and not trying for perfection. You can write about the weather, your classes, the people you meet, the place you live, the first time you see snow or your first baseball game, money, jobs, customs . . . You do not need to spend long periods of time on these passages, and they do not need to be perfect. Don't worry about mistakes. Think about your ideas and opinions. The purpose of freewriting is to develop *fluency* (the flow of language), not *accuracy* (exactness and correctness). You will do other assignments to develop accuracy.

A journal is also a special keepsake for the future. Months or years from now, it will help you to remember the events and emotions of this time of your life. Memories fade. Sometime in the future you will be thankful to have a record of your experiences. So, take the bull by the horns and start freewriting today.

In this course you are asked to keep a daily journal for freewriting—in English. From time to time your teacher may ask to look briefly at your journal to see how much you have written. At times you will be asked to choose one part to read to the class or to rewrite. It will be your choice and you will have time to make it perfect.

LEARNING STRATEGY

Overcoming Limitations: Focusing first on ideas, rather than accuracy, improves your writing.

TASK: PRACTICING FREEWRITING

In order to get in the mood for your personal journal, do some freewriting now. Use paper from your notebook. In the time given to you, write as much as you can about one of the following topics. (Or suggest another topic, if you want.) Your teacher will tell you when to begin. Write fast in English until you are told to stop. Do not worry about correct spelling or making sense. Do not worry about perfection. You will not be graded on correctness. The goal is to write *many words*. The goal is fluency. Do not stop the flow!

SOME POSSIBLE TOPICS

1. An Important Person in My Life
2. The Best Book I Ever Read
3. Building a House
4. How to Buy a Car
5. A Garden in the Spring
6. My Favorite Restaurant

THEME 5: THE NORTH AMERICAN CLASSROOM

The system of education in North America is different from the system in many other countries. In those countries, education is centralized. It is controlled by one group of people, often from the capital. In the United States and Canada, education is controlled on a local level. Even in the same state, province, or city, there can be schools, institutes, or universities with very different ways of teaching.

Left: A North American classroom in the 1940s.
Right: A North American classroom in the 1990s.

TASK 1: THEN AND NOW

In the last 50 years there have been great changes in North American classrooms. Look at the two photos. One is from the 1940s; the other from the 1990s. How many differences do you see between the past and the present? Write down a list of differences. Compare with your classmates.

TASK 2: OUTSIDE ASSIGNMENT: MAKING OBSERVATIONS

If possible, go on an observation tour in a school, university, or institute.* Go alone or with another student. Take a notebook. Write down your observations. Go into classes, if you are allowed, and sit in the back. Answer these questions about each class. Also write down any other unusual or interesting details. Afterwards, return to class and report on what you saw.

1. Clothing. What is the teacher wearing? The students?
2. Speaking/Listening. Who is talking? Who is listening? What percentage of the time for each?
3. Movement. Who is moving? How much? In what ways?
4. Arrangement. How are the desks arranged? Are they in the traditional way, as in the photos of the 1940s? Or are they similar to the photos from the 1990s?
5. Noise. What noises do you hear?
6. Teaching Style. Are students learning details by heart? Are they working in small groups? Is there a class discussion?
7. Other Observations . . .

---

*If this kind of visit is not possible, watch a video about North American education.

Forming Concepts: Analyzing the similarities and differences between two items gives you a better understanding of both.

TASK 3: FINDING SIMILARITIES AND DIFFERENCES IN SYSTEMS OF EDUCATION

Look at the following charts. They contain statements about university systems. Think about the statements. Do they describe the system in your culture? Do you think they describe the system in North America? Then write *yes* in the correct place. If you think they do not describe the system, write *no.* If you are not sure, write *unsure,* or write a comment to explain. Compare answers with your classmates. Find out from your teacher if you are right about the North American system.

CHART 1:   Student-Teacher Relationship at Colleges and Universities

DESCRIPTION	YOUR CULTURE	NORTH AMERICAN CULTURE
1. The teacher and students may make decisions together about the class.	_____	_____
2. There is a lot of class discussion.	_____	_____
3. Students frequently ask questions in class.	_____	_____
4. Some teachers are called by their first names.	_____	_____
5. Many teachers dress in casual (not formal) clothes.	_____	_____
6. Teachers sometimes sit on their desks in the classroom.	_____	_____
7. Some students wear jeans or shorts to class.	_____	_____
8. Students work in pairs or groups in class.	_____	_____
9. Students sometimes have social events with teachers.	_____	_____
10. Many teachers are women.	_____	_____

Threads

The average number of days in the U.S. school year for elementary and high school is 180. This compares with 180 in Sweden and Mexico. Belgium has 160; Canada has 195–200; Scotland has 200; Israel has 215; South Korea has 220; and Japan has 243.

CHART 2: Coursework at Colleges and Universities

DESCRIPTION	YOUR CULTURE	NORTH AMERICAN CULTURE
1. Class attendance is not important.	_____	_____
2. All information for a course comes from textbooks.	_____	_____
3. Students learn course material by heart.	_____	_____
4. Short quizzes are not given.	_____	_____
5. All tests come at the end of the term or year.	_____	_____
6. Tests cover large amounts of information.	_____	_____
7. Many exams are oral.	_____	_____
8. Written objective tests, such as multiple choice or true/false, are not used.	_____	_____

TASK 4: TALKING IT OVER

1. Which chart has more descriptions related to the system of your culture?
2. Which chart has more descriptions related to the North American system?
3. In your opinion, what are the main differences between the North American education system and the system of your culture? What other information would you need to get to support your idea?
4. What similarities are there between the two systems? What other information would you need to get to support this idea?

TASK 5: BRAINSTORMING ABOUT THE COURSE

Think about the following aspects of the course. Talk about them.

a. The four basic skills: reading, writing, speaking, listening. Which do you like best? Which is most important for you?
b. Tests and exams. Should they be oral or written? Do you like multiple choice, true/false, matching, fill-in-the-blanks? Do you like short-answer or essay tests? A combination?
c. What about homework? How many hours of homework do you do each night? What kind of homework should it be?
d. Is it good to do oral reports (talk in front of the whole class)? If people are afraid to do this, do we say, "Don't worry! Just develop a thick skin!"

Give your opinions on these questions or on other points. If you like, write down your opinion. Read it to the class when it is your turn.

What suggestions do you have about the course you are taking? A suggestion is a recommendation, a piece of advice. For example, *Teach us how to take True/False tests* is a suggestion. Or you may ask a question, like *Do I have to work in groups?* Write out at least one suggestion or question and put it into the Suggestion/Question Box, or give it to your teacher.

THEME 6: WHAT DOES IT MEAN TO *ADJUST*?

When you speak a new language, do you acquire a new personality? It seems like a funny question. But think for a moment about how people look when they are speaking: French . . . Chinese . . . Spanish . . . Russian . . . Korean . . . English . . . Inuit . . . Swedish . . . German . . . Japanese. . . . Their faces are different. They move their hands and bodies differently too. If you learn to speak English well, will you change inside? If so, is that good or bad? Can you learn English and *not* change?

When you come to live in a new culture, there are three possible ways of acting.

Threads

Through time and space
I travel
Seeking these two alone:
The SAVOR of the
strange,
The SOLACE of the
known.

Sara Teasdale, American poet
(1884–1933)

THE THREE POSSIBLE WAYS OF ACTING IN A NEW CULTURE

1. Try to stay exactly the same. Keep yourself pure. Accept the customs that are necessary. But do not change your way of thinking. Do not get contaminated by other ways. Do not lose who you are. Think: "That's the American, or Canadian, way. That is not my way."
2. Try to become like people in the new culture. Forget your old habits and ways of thinking. Forget the customs of your culture. Take them off like old clothing. Imitate what you see. Blend in so you seem like everyone else. Become someone new. Say to yourself, "I belong here."
3. Stay the same in some ways and change in other ways. Observe what you see. Try some new customs and habits. Think about new ideas. Take what you like and reject (don't accept) what you don't like. Change some of your ways of thinking, but keep others. Mix together the old and the new.

LEARNING STRATEGY

Understanding and Using Emotions: Expressing your opinions gives you a chance to practice speaking and clarify your ideas.

TASK 1: EXPRESSING YOUR OPINIONS

1. What are the advantages (good points) of the first way of acting?
2. What are its disadvantages (bad points)?
3. What are the advantages of the second way of acting?
4. What are its disadvantages?
5. What are the advantages of the third way of acting?
6. What are its disadvantages?
7. Are all of the ways of acting really *adjusting?*
8. In your opinion, which of the three ways is best? Or does that depend on the circumstances? Explain your answer.

TASK 2: PLAYING WITH OPTICAL ILLUSIONS

There is an old saying in English, "Seeing is believing." That is often true, but it doesn't apply to optical illusions. An optical illusion is a drawing that fools us by giving a wrong impression. Look at these three optical illusions. Try to answer the questions. The correct answers are in the Answer Appendix at the end of the book.

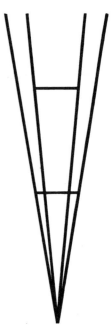

Optical Illusion 1: Point of View
Look carefully at the two horizontal (back and forth) lines. Which one is longer: the top one or the bottom one?

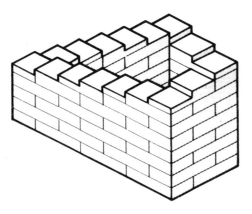

Optical Illusion 2: Upstairs Downstairs
Find the top step. When (and *if*) you find it, start looking for the bottom step!

Optical Illusion 3: Straight and Narrow
How many of the vertical (up and down) lines are bending this way and that? And how many of them are perfectly straight?

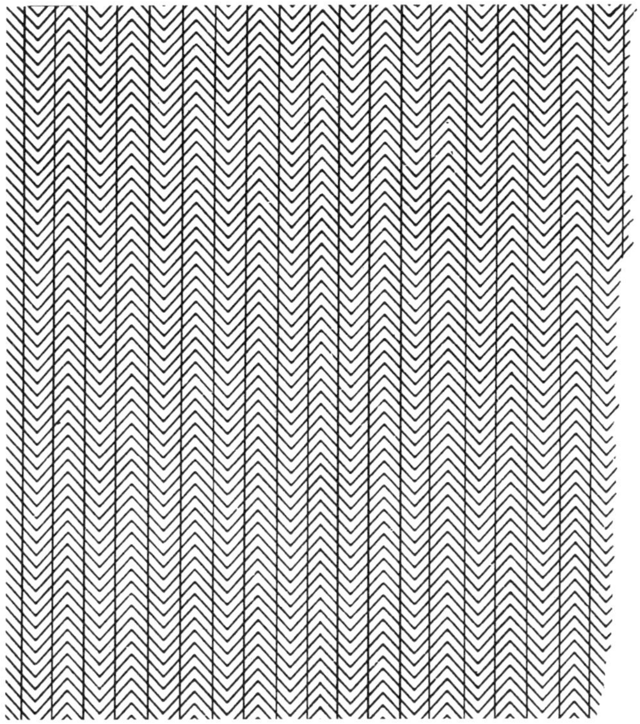

ANSWERING AN OPEN-ENDED QUESTION

Some questions do not have one right answer. They can be answered in several ways. Think of an answer for the following question. Compare answers with your classmates.
Why are optical illusions like adjusting to a new culture?

_____

_____

_____

_____

What Can We Say to Someone New?

INTRODUCTION

The moment of truth: another person walks up to you. Maybe the person is a stranger, or someone you know only a little. What do you say? Where do you look? Who speaks first? When we are young, we learn to speak with our families, relatives, and friends. When we grow older, we learn to speak with others. Each culture has its own way of greeting. Every language has special words for saying hello and goodbye, for starting a conversation, and for answering questions. This chapter presents ideas and practice for talking with North Americans.

Think about some goals for your own improvement.

To learn more about:

• Ways of saying hello and goodbye
• Common gestures and "body language" in North America
• Polite and impolite questions, and how they vary from culture to culture
• Ways to ask and answer questions with people we meet

To practice skills:

• Using context to make intelligent guesses
• Finding differences and similarities
• Observing gestures and movements
• Writing freely in a journal
• Scanning for information

To acquire new vocabulary

THEME 1: MEETING AND GREETING IN THE UNITED STATES AND CANADA

Americans and Canadians like to appear friendly. On the street, in school or at work, they smile and say hello to others. Bosses, employees, classmates, teachers—it doesn't matter who speaks first. People look directly at the other person and greet him or her. Here are some common greetings. Listen to your teacher read them. Say each greeting aloud.

Good morning, Mrs. Anderson. How are you today?

Good evening.* How are you?

---

*"Good night" is not used as a greeting. It is used to say good-bye to someone at night.

Hi, Tom! How is it going? (How's it going?)

Hello. How are you doing? (How're you doin'?)

In The United States and Canada, people do not expect a long answer. They say something brief. The other person says something brief. Then they go on their way. If the two people have stopped walking, usually one will mention the need to leave. Then both people will say goodbye. Listen to these common answers. Then repeat them.

Fine, thank you. How are you?	Just fine thanks.
I'm doing well, thanks. How about you? (How 'bout you?)	Great, thank you.
Very well, thank you, very busy.	Yes, me too. Nice to see you. Goodbye.
Well, have to go now. So long.	See you later.
I guess it's time to go back to work.	Nice talking with you.
Bye, now.	Bye!

Threads

The word *goodbye* is a contraction (shortened form) of the very old expression *God be with ye,* used hundreds of years ago in England.

TASK 1: TALKING IT OVER

1. What are some different ways of saying hello?
2. Which greeting do you use only at night?
3. Which two greetings are very informal? Why?
4. Is it correct to say a person's name in a greeting? Is it necessary?
5. Do you know other greetings in English? Who uses them? (Teenagers? Older people?)
6. What are some different ways of saying goodbye?
7. Look at the photo on page 21. In your opinion, what is the man saying? And the woman? Make up a short conversation. Write it down. Compare answers with your classmates.

LEARNING STRATEGY

Overcoming Limitations: Role-playing is a good way to practice social skills and new expressions.

TASK 2: SAYING HELLO AND GOODBYE

According to an old saying, "Practice makes perfect." Say all the greetings and answers again. Then work with a partner and act out these situations. Take turns playing each role. (If you do not feel ready to work with a partner, write a dialogue for one situation.)

1. You are walking down the street. You see your teacher, Mr. Hill. You greet him and he answers, but you do not stop.
2. Your name is Anthony (or Angela). You work in the office of a big hospital. You go to the supermarket and see your boss, Miss Chung, there. You stop to talk. Then you say goodbye.
3. Your name is Maria (or Mario). You are on your way to class and meet a schoolmate, Jo Anne (or John). You greet each other and then stop to talk a while. You are in a hurry to get back to your studies or work. So you make an excuse. Then you say goodbye.

TASK 3: OBSERVING HELLOS AND GOODBYES

Make a list of different ways to say hello and goodbye in English. Try to include as many different words and phrases as possible, such as formal ones, slang, and jokes. Write comments after the expressions about how to use them. To find these, ask others for help, listen to people, watch television or look in a book in the library. Your teacher may ask you to read an expression from your list.

THEME 2: MEETING AND GREETING IN DIFFERENT CULTURES

Americans and Canadians are often surprised by the greetings in other cultures. Some seem long and complicated, not like the plain style of North America. A translation of the words doesn't help. On the other hand, many people from other cultures find North American greetings strange, even rude. We have to look below the surface to understand the differences and similarities in greetings.

A. Different Styles of Greeting: An Example

Read this brief selection from the book *Baghdad without a Map*. It gives a *specific* (particular) example of different styles of greetings. The book is by an American working and traveling in the Middle East.

GET READY TO READ: GUESSING THE MEANINGS OF WORDS

Many times you can guess the meaning of a word from its context. *Context* means the words around it. Find the following words in the reading selection. Choose the correct meanings. Then read the selection.

1. _____ abrupt
   a. long and full of details
   b. too brief and not polite
   c. good and proper

2. _____ jasmine
   a. a type of flower
   b. a special place
   c. a happy feeling

Greetings in Egypt

by Tony Horowitz

In Egypt it is considered abrupt to begin any conversation without at least half of the following:
Good morning.
Good morning to you.
Good morning of light.
Good morning of roses.
Good morning of jasmines (and so on, through the rest of the garden).
And how are you?
Fine, and you?
Fine also, thanks be to God.
Thanks to God.
Welcome, most welcome.
Welcome to you.

LEARNING STRATEGY

Forming Concepts: Guessing the meanings of new words improves your vocabulary without constantly using a dictionary.

TASK: TALKING IT OVER

1. How are Egyptian greetings different from North American greetings?

2. Which explanation(s) for these differences do you think is best?

   _____ climate   _____ work habits

   _____ language structure   _____ rules of courtesy

   _____ religious beliefs   _____ other (Explain.)

3. In your opinion, how would North Americans feel about Egyptian greetings? Why?

4. Think about an Egyptian who comes to Canada or the U.S.A. How would he or she feel about North American greetings? Why?

B. Similarities Among Greeting Styles: A General View

At first glance, we see the differences between North American and Egyptian greetings. But they are also similar. They both use "formulas," set phrases with expected answers. All cultures have formulas for greetings. Read the following examples and guess which answers are the expected ones. (The correct information is in the Answer Appendix at the end of the book.)

1. _____ (American/Canadian) "Hi, how are you?"
   a. "Fine, thanks, and you?"
   b. "I'm tired and my feet hurt."

2. _____ (Egyptian) "Good morning of roses."
   a. "Good morning of jasmines."
   b. "Good morning of problems."

3. _____ (Chinese) "Have you eaten yet?"
   a. "Yes, I've eaten, and you?"
   b. "No, I skipped breakfast today."

4. _____ (Thai) "Where are you going?"
   a. "To do some errands, and you?"
   b. "To look for a job."

5. _____ (Certain African groups) "Are you alive?"
   a. "Yes, I am alive, and you?"
   b. "Of course, I am! Don't you see me?"

TASK 1: TALKING IT OVER

1. What is similar about all five greetings?
2. What is "wrong" with the unexpected answers?
3. Think about greetings in your culture. Are they similar to any of the examples? How would you translate them into English? What are the expected answers? What would be an unexpected answer?
4. Rules have exceptions. Sometimes we *do* use unexpected answers to greetings. In your opinion, when does this happen? With whom? Why?

TASK 2: LEARNING NEW GREETINGS

Write "Hello" and "How are you?" and the common answers in your native language. Take turns giving greetings in your native languages. Explain to the class what the words mean.

TASK 3: COMMUNICATION BREAKDOWN

Read the following opinion. It is from Tanya, a Russian woman living in Canada. Then write answers to the questions. Compare answers with your classmates.

Tanya: "Everyone says that Canadians are friendly but I think this is false. I work in a laboratory. Often I meet Canadians in the hallway and ask them how they are. They always say, *Fine, thank you.* I don't believe they are always fine. They ask me how I am. I start to talk, but they don't listen. Soon they say, *Well, see you later!* Why do they ask, *How are you?* They don't really want to know."

1. What does Tanya think about Canadians? Why?
2. What caused a problem with communication?
3. How can Tanya improve her communication with Canadians?

YOUR PERSONAL JOURNAL: COMPARING AND CONTRASTING

Think about some aspect of your culture, for example, the houses, the schools, the streets, the stores, or the clothing. How is it similar to North American culture? How is it different? Practice comparing and contrasting by listing the similarities (points that are similar) and differences (points that are different) in your journal, following this model.

A Comparison of _____ in Canada (or the United States) and in

_____.

SIMILARITIES	DIFFERENCES
1. _____	1. _____
_____	_____
2. _____	2. _____
_____	_____
3. _____	3. _____
_____	_____
(You can continue the numbers if you have more points.)	

IT WORKS!
Learning Strategy:
Looking for
Similarities and
Differences

After you make your list, answer the following questions: Do you prefer your own culture's way or the North American way? Why? Are there some good points to both ways? In your opinion, do most people prefer their own culture's ways or other ways? Why? Your teacher may ask for volunteers to read their comparisons or answers.

We talk without words in many ways. One way is through "body language." Every culture has certain gestures (body movements) with a meaning. The meanings are not the same in every culture.

One North American gesture for *O.K., Great!* is very common in the United States and Canada. In Japan the same gesture means *money,* and in some other cultures it has a rude, insulting meaning. From this we can see that the rudeness is not in the gesture itself. The rudeness is in the wish of someone to insult another person.

TASK 1: GUESSING THE MEANING

How well can you read body language? Look at the following photos and at the list called Meanings of Common North American Gestures. Try to guess what each photo means. Your teacher may give you some hints

and then tell you if you are right. Practice making these gestures and saying what they mean.

MEANINGS OF COMMON NORTH AMERICAN GESTURES

Come here.	O.K. (Great!)	Be quiet.
I don't know.	Naughty, naughty.	Good-bye.
Stop! Slow down.	No more, please.	A little bit.
Big trouble (dead)!	What did you say?	Thumbs up. (Great!)

TASK 2: WHAT ARE YOU TRYING TO TELL ME?

(For a class with students from different cultures)

Turn to the person next to you and make the sign that means "Come here" in your culture. Then, go around once again, making another gesture. How many different ways can you show the same meaning? Are there some gestures that work for several cultures?

(For a class with students from the same culture)

Which of the meanings on the list have gestures in your culture? Which do not? Are some of the same gestures used in North America and in your culture?

THEME 4: BODY LANGUAGE AND MEETING NEW PEOPLE

Body language is important for meeting people all over the world. The following selection is from the book, *The Most Popular Gestures* by the American businessman and writer, Roger Axtell. It describes some gestures used in greetings around the world: the bow, the handshake, the hug, the namaste, the salaam, the pat on the back. Do you know how to do any of these? You will learn more about them in the reading.

GET READY TO READ: SCANNING FOR EXACT WORDS

English uses quotation marks to show the exact words of people. Look at the reading selection and practice using quotation marks.

1. Lines 1–2. The author's father used to give him advice. Write down the exact words of his father:

_____

How do you know these were his exact words?

2. Think of something (about any topic) that *your* father or mother used to say. Write down the exact words in English:

_____

Did you use the correct punctuation?

3. In your language, how do you show someone's exact words?

_____

GET READY TO READ:
VOCABULARY RELATING TO THE BODY

English has many verbs and nouns to express movements of the body. Look at the following words from the reading selection. Tell which body part(s) can make these movements. Then make short sentences for each movement. You can use the noun or the verb.

EXAMPLE: 7. (hands) His *handshake* is very strong.

1. bend (n., v.)
2. bow (n., v.)
3. clap (n., v.)
4. embrace (n., v.)
5. extend (v.)
6. grip (n., v.)

7. handshake (n.)
8. hug (n., v.)
9. nod (n., v.)
10. pray (n., v.)
11. shake (hands) (v.)
12. stare (n., v.)

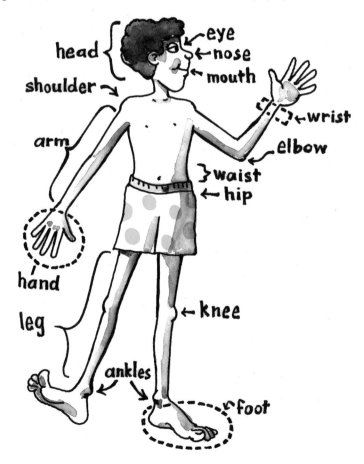

The most popular gestures

by Roger Axtell

B. the *salaam*

When you shake hands," my father used to say to me, "be sure you give 'em a good, firm grip. Also, look 'em straight in the eye."

I didn't know that in other parts of the world fathers were teaching their sons and daughters something very different.

For example, fathers in India were teaching their children the *namaste* (A). The namaste is done with hands in a praying position, and a small bow. It also means "thank you" and "I'm sorry." In Thailand, this same gesture is called the *wai.*

A. the *namaste*

There are other forms of greetings as well. In the Middle East, the older generation still gives the *salaam.* In this signal, the right hand moves upward. First it touches the heart, then the forehead and then moves outward, with a slight nod of the head. (B). The words with this greeting are, *salaam alaykum,* meaning, "Peace be with you."

Let's return to the more familiar gesture of greeting, the handshake. While *my* father was teaching me "Firm handshake, direct eye con-tact," fathers in the Middle East were teaching their sons "When you shake hands, a *gentle* grip is appropriate. Don't grip the hand firmly. A firm grip shows aggression." And in Japan and Korea, fathers were saying, "Yes, gentle, not firm, and try to avoid direct eye contact. Staring at someone is disrespectful."

Among North Americans and many Europeans, gripping a limp hand is distasteful. To them it is like "gripping a dead fish."

Some people believe Americans go too far in the other direction, however. Prince Charles of England must be an expert on greetings by now, and he has complained of the finger-crunching grip of the Americans. "Especially Texans," he adds.

C. the *abrazo*

In Northern Europe, you generally receive a short, firm, one-pump handshake. Also, women and chil-dren there will usually extend their hand in greeting. But in North America and in the Far East, women will only occasionally do this. The same is true for children.

In Latin American countries, the hug is called the *abrazo,* which means "embrace." It is often accom-

D. the bow

panied by a couple of hearty claps on the back (C). Most North Americans, Northern Europeans, and Orientals find this touching or hugging very uncomfortable.

Now let us turn to the most courtly of all greetings, the *bow.* Western business people working in Japan are very careful to imitate the Japanese. But they also joke: "You know you've been in Japan too long when you have a telephone conversation and you bow into the telephone" (D).

TASK 1: MATCHING

Match the greeting to the people who use it.

1. ____ the bow	**a.** Latin Americans
2. ____ the *namaste*	**b.** Texans
3. ____ the *wai*	**c.** Japanese
4. ____ the one-pump handshake	**d.** Middle Easterners
5. ____ the finger-crunching handshake	**e.** People from Thailand
6. ____ the *abrazo*	**f.** Northern Europeans
7. ____ the *salaam*	**g.** Indians

TASK 2: CHECKING COMPREHENSION

1. What can the *namaste* mean?
2. What words go with the *salaam*?
3. Which fathers prefer a gentle handshake? Why?
4. Which fathers prefer a firm handshake? Why?
5. Should we have direct eye contact during the handshake?
6. What is a limp hand like to North Americans and many Europeans?
7. Can you shake hands like a Texan?
8. Why are some people uncomfortable with Latin American greetings?
9. What happens to Western business people in Japan after a long time?

LEARNING STRATEGY

Managing Your Learning: Scanning helps you find specific information.

TASK 3: SCANNING FOR ANTONYMS*

Scanning is a useful reading skill. We use it to find small bits of information. To scan, move your eyes quickly and stop only at the information you want. Scan the reading to find antonyms for the following words. They are in order from the beginning to the end.

1. gentle _____	6. respectful _____
2. younger _____	7. pleasant _____
3. downward _____	8. false _____
4. war _____	9. comfortable _____
5. indirect _____	10. careless _____

_____

*Remember that antonyms are words that mean the opposite of something. An antonym of *good* is *bad*. An antonym of *small* is *big*.

TASK 4: FINDING PREFIXES THAT MEAN "NOT"

Prefixes are letters attached to the front of words. They change the meaning of the word. *Lucky* means one thing. ***Unlucky*** means just the opposite, *not lucky. Un-* is a prefix that means *not.*

1. What antonym from the exercise "Scan for Antonyms" uses the prefix *un-*?

2. What other prefixes in the exercise mean "not"?

3. Make antonyms for the following words by adding *-un* and use these antonyms in short sentences.

   a. known

   _____

   _____

   b. usual

   _____

   _____

   c. happy

   _____

   _____

   d. welcome

   _____

   _____

   e. clear

   _____

   _____

   f. common

   _____

   _____

TASK 5: PLEASED TO MEET YOU!

Work with a partner. Take turns greeting each other with at least two different styles from around the world. Then practice introducing yourself and shaking hands, North American style.

EXAMPLE: "Hi. My name is _____ _____. What's your name?"
"My name is _____ _____."
(Then shake hands and say . . .)
"How do you do?"
"Pleased to meet you."

After you finish, change partners and begin again.

Go on a personal observation tour. Go alone or with one or more classmates. Find a comfortable place to sit and watch people, such as a cafeteria, shopping center, train station or park. If you cannot observe English-speaking people directly, watch a television show or a movie. Make comparisons with your culture. Record your observations.

1. How close do people sit to each other? How close do they stand when they are talking? Are they closer or farther away than people in your culture in the same situations?
2. Do English-speaking people move their hands or heads while they talk? What kinds of gestures or movements do you see? Are these similar to those of your culture? Explain.
3. Who makes more gestures? Men or women? Older people or younger people? Or is there no difference? Is this the same in your culture?
4. Do the people touch each other during their conversations? How? When? Explain. Is this similar or different to your own culture?

You may be asked to share your answers with your classmates. Perhaps a chart can be made on the board to compare observations from the whole class. In two or three months, you may look back at this journal entry with surprise. As you observe more, your ideas may change.

THEME 5: HOW TO START A CONVERSATION

Threads

A smile goes a long way. First impressions are important.

English sayings

You go to a house for dinner. The host gives you a drink and says, "Please sit down." Then what? Canadian social customs are informal and direct. American customs are even more so. In both countries, people ask questions right away. They expect you to answer and to ask questions too. Of course, you do not want to ask the wrong questions. Some questions are polite. Some are not. The idea of politeness varies from culture to culture.

The next reading selection is from the book *Living in the U.S.A.* by Alison R. Lanier. It talks about personal questions. Before starting it, do the following exercises to help your comprehension.

Look at the questions. In your culture, are these polite (courteous) questions for a first meeting? Write *P* after questions that are polite, in your culture, *NP* after questions that are not polite. If you are uncertain about some questions, write *U.*

1. _____ How old are you?

2. _____ Where are you from?

3. _____ How much did you pay for your shirt?

4. _____ Do you play tennis well?

5. _____ What do you do (for a living)?

6. _____ Does your mother work outside the home?

7. _____ Do you have any brothers and sisters?

8. _____ Are you married?

9. _____ How much do you pay for rent?

10. _____ Where do you live?

11. _____ How many children do you have?

12. _____ How do you like this weather?

13. _____ What is your religion?

14. _____ What is your salary?

15. _____ Do you live alone?

16. _____ What does your father do for a living?

17. _____ What do you think of this city?

18. _____ Why don't you have any children?

Every one of these questions is polite for a first meeting in at least one culture. In some cultures, most of them are impolite (not polite). In North America, most of these questions are polite. Six are *im*polite. Two others are questionable. (They are considered impolite by some Americans and many Canadians.) Compare your answers with those of your classmates. Why did you mark *U* after some questions? Try to guess which questions are not polite in the United States. You will find this information in the reading.

GET READY TO READ:
LEARNING THE MEANING OF IDIOMS

Look at the box on the next page and learn the idioms. Two of them are important for understanding the reading selection.

Three Idioms

Idioms are groups of words that say one thing and mean something different. Look at the idioms and the pictures. The pictures show what the words say. Try to guess the meanings by reading the sentences. The answers are in the Answer Appendix at the end of the book.

1. to break the ice
At parties or meetings, people sometimes use a game or activity to break the ice.

*IT WORKS!
Learning Strategy:
Visualizing New
Vocabulary*

2. to look for common ground
In their contract discussions, the boss and employees are looking for common ground.

3. to get the point
The man listened to the explanation, but he didn't get the point.

Now read the selection and learn some questions that are good for breaking the ice.

Personal questions

by Alison R. Lanier

Conversational questions may seem to you too personal and too numerous—especially when you first arrive.

"Where do you work?" "How many children do you have?" "Do you play golf?" "What is your score?" "Have you taken your vacation yet?" are not personal questions by American standards. They are a search for common ground. Understand that such questions are meant to be friendly. The questioner is interested in you.

Many of us move around the country often. We meet many people. By rapid questioning we establish an easy understanding.

In less mobile countries people operate on a different basis. They wait until there has been time to get to know the newcomer. Only then do they feel comfortable in discussing anything personal. Americans move faster, living like a movie that is run at double speed. Tomorrow they may be transferred across the country or you may be back across the sea. "If we flow apart again, we will at least have had today," say the Americans.

To those coming from other countries, the American way can seem abrupt and frightening. Yet even here some subjects are not mentioned. They are considered too personal and impolite. These include questions about a person's age, financial affairs, cost of clothes or personal belongings, religion, love (or sex) life, and about why you don't have children.

If you are asked questions which seem too personal, you need not answer them. You can simply smile and say pleasantly that you do not know or "In my country that would be a funny question." Then follow it quickly with another topic. The American will not be offended, but he will get the point.

—*Living in the U.S.A.*

TASK 1: CHECKING COMPREHENSION

Choose the correct way to finish each sentence about the reading.

1. Americans ask many questions of a newcomer because
   a. they don't care about people's feelings.
   b. they want to find common ground.
   c. they fear people who are different.

2. The reading compares the rhythm of American life to
   a. a boat on the waves of the sea.
   b. a train going through a tunnel.
   c. a movie run at double speed.

3. American life is more _____ than life in many other countries.
   a. mobile   b. friendly   c. impolite

4. Americans move fast to make new friends because
   a. they want to finish the conversation and go to work.
   b. they often are transferred and have to leave old friends.
   c. they are nervous about talking to people from other cultures.

5. Someone asks you very personal questions. You do not want to answer them. You should
   a. keep quiet and say nothing.
   b. answer them completely as well as you can. After all, you are in *their* country.
   c. tell them, "It's none of your business!"
   d. say "I don't know" or "That's a funny question," and change the subject.

TASK 2: LEARNING VOCABULARY THROUGH WORD FAMILIES

Adjectives are descriptive words. By adding different endings (suffixes), you change some nouns into adjectives. Both words are in the same word family. They sound similar. Learn them together.

EXAMPLES: Objects that belong to a <u>person</u> are <u>personal</u> belongings.

A gesture that shows <u>respect</u> is a <u>respectful</u> gesture.

Complete the following sentences with the adjective from the reading. If you don't remember it, scan the reading for it. (Review directions for scanning on page 32.)

1. Questions used in a <u>conversation</u> are _____ questions.

2. Comments said to a <u>friend</u> are _____ comments.

3. A situation that gives us <u>comfort</u> is a _____ situation.

4. A custom that gives us a <u>fright</u> is a _____ custom.

5. Affairs dealing with money and <u>finance</u> are _____ affairs.

TASK 3: SCANNING FOR IMPORTANT WORDS

Scan the reading for the following words. They are in the order of appearance. Use each one in a short sentence.

1. A word meaning *fast* that starts with *r:* _____

2. A word meaning *full of movement and change* that starts with *m:* _____

3. A word meaning *someone who has just arrived* that starts with *n:* _____

4. A word meaning *sent to work in a different place.* It starts with *t:* _____

TASK 4: CHOOSING POLITE QUESTIONS

A. What are the six subjects that Americans consider impolite for questions? Scan for them in the reading and write them down.

1. _____   4. _____

2. _____   5. _____

3. _____   6. _____

B. Now look back at the questions in "Get Ready to Read" on page 34. Which questions are related to these six subjects? Which do you think are definitely impolite in the U.S.A.? Which are questionable? Compare opinions with your classmates.

TASK 5: REAL-LIFE SITUATIONS

Work alone or with one or two others. Write out a conversation for one of the following situations. Your teacher may call on you or your group to read your conversation to the class.

A. Talking with a "Shy Guy"

A business executive from another country is at a party in London, Ontario. A Canadian man comes up and introduces himself. Then he looks at his feet. He seems uncomfortable. The executive sees that he is very shy. She decides to break the ice. She introduces herself and tells where she is from. She says something nice about the weather or the party. Then she asks him two safe, friendly questions. Soon the Canadian man "warms up." He answers the questions and asks a few of his own. They find some common ground. (This may be adapted for two men or two women.)

B. Answering Impoliteness with Politeness

A student from another culture is living in Los Angeles, California, for one year. Mr. and Mrs. Carpenter invite the student to dinner "Just call us Ted and Sarah," they say. Then they hand out very strong drinks. Everyone sits in the living room. The Carpenters ask many questions. The first three are polite questions and the student answers. The student understands that they want to be friendly. Then they start to ask very personal questions. The student feels uncomfortable. The student answers with a short sentence, then changes the subject. The Carpenters get the point. Everyone talks about the new subject during dinner.

LEARNING STRATEGY

Understanding and Using Emotions: Writing about your feelings helps you understand yourself and others.

YOUR PERSONAL JOURNAL: DESCRIBING AN
EXPERIENCE FROM THE OUTSIDE AND THE INSIDE

Think about a time in your life when you felt uncomfortable in a social situation. Tell the story from the outside (the facts, telling *who, what, when, where,* and *why*). But also tell the story from the inside (your thoughts and feelings). Were you worried, nervous, angry, upset or unsure of yourself? Also, describe your feelings now, as you look back on it. Does it seem upsetting now? Or unimportant and funny?

Take a moment to look back at the goals for this chapter. Which ones did you do best in? It is difficult to measure progress in language skills and cultural awareness. However, the following exercises can help you review some of the key vocabulary presented in the chapter. (Answers are given in the Answer Appendix at the end of the book.)

VOCABULARY REVIEW: SYNONYMS

Match each word in the first column to its synonym in the second column.

1. ____ brief	**a.** rude
2. ____ common	**b.** embrace
3. ____ firm	**c.** fast
4. ____ gesture	**d.** short
5. ____ greet	**e.** salary
6. ____ hug	**f.** particular
7. ____ impolite	**g.** strong
8. ____ rapid	**h.** say hello
9. ____ specific	**i.** usual
	j. movement

VOCABULARY REVIEW: ANTONYMS

Give an antonym for each of the following words.

1. comfortable _____	**6.** friendly _____
2. disrespectful _____	**7.** hello _____
3. downward _____	**8.** courteous _____
4. firm _____	**9.** rudeness _____
5. formal _____	**10.** similarity _____

How Important Is a Name?

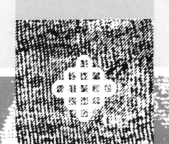

INTRODUCTION

There is an old saying that, basically, all people are the same. Individuals from all over the world have similar needs, emotions and ambitions. This is true, but so is the opposite. All people are different. To begin with, there is the difference between men and women. Then there are other divisions, like culture, language, family, and appearance. All these factors make up who we are, our identity. This chapter talks about names and customs, and how we form our identities.

Think about some goals for your own improvement.

To learn more about:

• Similarities and differences in the uses of names around the world
• The sounds and rhythm of English
• U.S. and Canadian names and their meanings
• How to pronounce and use names in North America
• What happens to women's names
• Some factors relating to our identities

To practice skills:

• Scanning for details on charts and in exercises
• Skimming for general ideas
• Listening to sounds and noticing differences
• Using titles to predict the subject of readings
• Expanding on ideas
• Comparing different points of view

To acquire new vocabulary

THEME 1: OUR NAMES AND IDENTITIES

Ask yourself: "Who am I?" You think of your name. Your name is part of your identity. Its sound and meaning come from your family, language and culture. Sometimes people keep their names when they come to study or work in a new culture. Sometimes they change their names, or simply pronounce them differently. Read about the following four students who came to study in the United States and Canada.

Student 1

My name is Loi Nguyen, and I'm from Viet Nam. Some people tell me to anglicize my name (change it to make it more English). They tell me to call myself *Larry* or *Lance.* But I don't want to. My family gave me my name. I am the same person wherever I go. When I meet someone new, I

say my name slowly and clearly. I repeat it several times until people understand. Some of my classmates have made a joke about my name. I study Law, so they say I'm going to be a *loiyer.* I don't care. Let them laugh. I am Loi.

Student 2

I'm Jacqueline Matahnbat from Thailand, and I am a student in microbiology. *Jacqueline* is the name I use here in North America. I always liked that name and enjoy using it. I use my real name, *Molvipah,* with my family and people from my culture. It is hard for people to say in English. So I decided to change it. I didn't like the way people looked at me during introductions. They made faces when they tried to pronounce my name. They never said it right. In English, I am Jacqueline.

Student 3

Hi, I am Jesús Jiménez García from Nicaragua. With my English friends, I am "Joe." I never chose to change my name. It just happened. For my friends it was difficult to say *Jesús.* They said it was like swearing. In English it sounds disrespectful to say "Jesus." That is not true in my culture. But now I call myself *Joe,* and I use only one last name, Jimenez, the one from my father. I think it will be easier to get a job with that name.

Student 4

My name is Malika and I'm from India. In the region I come from, we have only one name. We do not need a first and a last name. This caused problems here at first because North Americans think everyone must have a first and last name. So I invented a new name for myself: V. Malika. The "V" stands for *Victory,* one of my favorite English words. I sign that for my official name. With most people here, I say I am *Vicki.* My real friends and my family call me Malika.

TASK 1: TALKING IT OVER

1. How many of the students use their real names in English? How many use a different name?
2. Who chose to change to a different name? Why?
3. What do you think of this decision?
4. Who uses a different name because it "just happened"?
5. Why did it happen? What do you think of this change of name?
6. Who had only one name before coming to North America?
7. How many names do you have? Why?
8. Do you know any North American names that seem difficult or strange to people in your culture? Which ones? Why?

Ziggy: A Rumor in His Own Time

by Tom Wilson

TASK 2: CHOOSING AND DEFENDING AN OPINION

Read the following statements. Think about them. Check whether you agree or disagree. Then write out a brief explanation of what you think about each one and why. Be prepared to read your explanations to the class.

1. We should not change our names. It is best to use the name given to us by our family.

   _____ Agree.   _____ Disagree.   Why? _____

   _____

2. We should change our names in a new culture because it will help us to be accepted.

   _____ Agree.   _____ Disagree.   Why? _____

   _____

3. There is no right or wrong answer about changing names. It depends on the situation.

   _____ Agree.   _____ Disagree.   Why? _____

   _____

TASK 3: LEARNING NEW IDIOMS

Guessing the Meaning of Three New Idioms

Here are three idioms that will be used in the chapter. The drawings show what the words say. Read the sentences and guess the real meaning for each idiom. (The answers are in the Answer Appendix at the end of the book.)

1. to get (or keep) the ball rolling
Who will get the ball rolling by being the first volunteer? Don't stop talking. Keep the ball rolling!

2. to make a big deal (out of something)
People don't like to work with him because he makes a big deal out of every little problem.

3. to take it with a grain of salt
I read the new list of rules, but I think we should take them with a grain of salt.

*IT WORKS!
Learning Strategy:
Visualizing Idioms*

Write about your name and the names in your family. Do they have meanings? Are these names common in your culture? Are some names repeated? Tell about the meanings and how different family members feel about their names. Illustrate your description with a drawing of your family tree, like the one in the sketch, or a different kind of drawing. Write your name and those of your relatives in the right places. Your teacher may ask to see your writing.

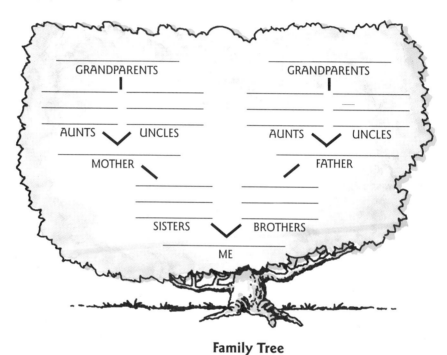

Family Tree

THEME 2: THE MOST POPULAR NAMES IN THE UNITED STATES AND CANADA

Names rise and fall with popularity. Some people like common names and others unusual ones. Let's look at common North American names and how they change.

A. A Chart of the Most Popular North American Names

The chart on page 48 gives the most popular names in North America in the 1950s and the 1990s. Before reading it, do the following exercises.

GET READY TO READ:
PRACTICING THE RHYTHM OF ENGLISH

Say your name aloud, in a normal way. Now, try to say your name with a very strong American or Canadian accent. Then do the same for the name of the town or city where you were born. Does the sound change each time? If so, how does it change?

Music has rhythm. Jazz sounds different from classical music. Languages have different rhythms too. We must listen to the sounds of a new language to hear its rhythm. We must imitate.

English has an *irregular rhythm.* Some syllables are stressed and some are unstressed. Stressed syllables are long, high, and loud. They usually keep their true vowel sound. Unstressed syllables are short, low, and quiet. They usually change their vowel sound to "uh" or "er." Every word has at least *one* stressed syllable. Compare the following words. Listen to how your teacher says them. How are the vowel sounds different in the first and second words? Why?

1. pot   potato   (*o* sounds like . . . then . . .)
2. mad   Madonna   (*a* sounds like . . . then . . .)
3. record (noun) record (verb)   (*e* sounds like . . . then . . .)
4. enter   listen   (*e* sound like . . . then . . .)

GET READY TO READ: HEARING THE DIFFERENCE
BETWEEN STRESSED AND UNSTRESSED SYLLABLES

How do you know which part of the word to stress in a word with more than one syllable? You must guess. There are no fixed rules. You must imitate what you hear. Many many names in English have stress on the first syllable. Practice saying the names below. *Exaggerate the first syllable.* It is the stressed syllable in all of these names. Make your voice higher. Stretch out the vowel sound. Make it louder.

Abraham	Lincoln	Abraham Lincoln
Michael	Jordan	Michael Jordan
Alice	Munro	Alice Munro
William	Shakespeare	William Shakespeare
Julia	Roberts	Julia Roberts
Agatha	Christie	Agatha Christie
Wayne	Gretzky	Wayne Gretzky
Robert	Redford	Robert Redford

Now look at the chart of common first names. Listen to your teacher pronounce them. Notice which syllable is stressed in each word. (When necessary, put an arrow over the vowel of the stressed syllable.) Repeat the names aloud.

EXAMPLES: Elizabeth   Amanda   Nicole   Danielle

Most Popular First Names in Canada and the United States
(in order of popularity)

	FOR GIRLS		FOR BOYS	
	1950s	1990s	1950s	1990s
1.	Mary	Jessica	John	Michael
2.	Elizabeth	Ashley	William	Christopher
3.	Barbara	Amanda	Charles	Matthew
4.	Dorothy	Jennifer	James	David
5.	Helen	Sarah	George	Daniel
6.	Margaret	Stephanie	Robert	Joshua
7.	Ruth	Nicole	Thomas	Andrew
8.	Virginia	Brittany	Henry	James
9.	Jean	Heather	Joseph	Robert
10.	Frances	Melissa	Edward	Ryan
11.	Nancy	Megan	Samuel	John
12.	Patricia	Elizabeth	Frank	Joseph
13.	Jane	Amber	Richard	Brandon
14.	Alice	Lauren	Harry	Jason
15.	Joan	Danielle	Francis	Justin
16.	Betty	Michelle	Frederick	Jonathan
17.	Dolores	Christina	Walter	Nicholas
18.	Eleanor	Crystal	David	Anthony
19.	Anne	Laura	Arthur	William
20.	Florence	Kimberly	Albert	Eric

TASK 1: SCANNING A CHART

Scan for the following bits of information. (Remember to move your eyes quickly and stop only at the information you want.) How long does it take to find the answers? Time yourself. How many minutes? _____ minutes.

1. The number of boys' names that begin with *R*: _____

2. The number of girls' names that begin with *L*: _____

3. The longest name on the chart (11 letters): _____

TASK 2: USING SCANNING FOR A TRUE/FALSE EXERCISE

To do some exercises, it is not necessary to read carefully. You only want some bits of information. So you scan for it. Read each item. Then scan the chart for the information. Write *T* for true or *F* for false before each item. The first person to finish, with correct answers, wins the prize.

1. _____ There are more girl's names of one syllable than boy's names of one syllable.

2. _____ Names of one syllable were more common in the 1950s than now.

3. _____ Two names of four syllables are on the chart.

4. _____ There are two girl's names with the stress on the second syllable.

5. _____ More boy's names have stayed popular than girl's names.

6. _____ No name on the chart begins with *I* or *P.*

7. _____ The most common letter to begin a name is *A.*

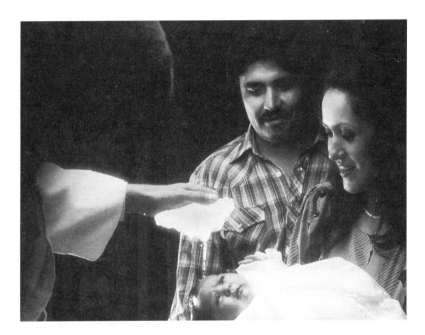

Many Christians bring their babies to church for baptism, a religious ceremony that gives the baby a name.

TASK 3: WHAT'S YOUR OPINION?

1. What names are difficult to pronounce? Which are easy?
2. Are any names similar to names in your culture?
3. Some names have songs about them: *Michelle; Ma Belle; Hey Jude; Angie; Sweet Georgia Brown; Danny Boy; Michael, Row the Boat Ashore;* etc. What names in your culture have songs about them?
4. In your culture, can you tell if a name is a man's name or a woman's name? How?
5. Which English names do you like best for women? For men?
6. Are there lucky names and unlucky names? Why or why not?

IT WORKS!
Learning Strategy:
Expressing Your
Opinion

B. Some Different Uses of Names and Nicknames

Threads

Father calls me William,
Sister calls me Will,
Mother calls me Willie,
But the fellers call me
—Bill!

From "Jest 'Fore Christmas" by
Eugene Field, American poet
(1850–1895)

In some cultures it is common to use titles when talking to people who are not family or friends. Sometimes these titles show a person's profession. Or they tell us that he or she is older and should be honored. In general, North Americans are not very formal; they are casual. That is true with titles too. In everyday life, titles are not used, except for Doctor (Dr.) for a medical doctor, and sometimes Professor (Prof.) for a university professor.

Naturally, Mr. and Mrs., Miss, and the newer form Ms. (pronounced *Miz,* and used for any woman, married or not) are used sometimes. (For example, these are used on the outside of the envelope when sending letters.) But people in the United States and Canada are so casual nowadays that they often use first names right away after meeting. In fact, many times even a boss or older person will ask you to use his or her first name or even a nickname.

Many North American names have nicknames. These are sometimes used by family and friends to show affection. *Liz, Beth,* and *Betty* are all common nicknames for the same name: *Elizabeth.*

Often nicknames are shorter than full names, such as *Hank* for Henry, or *Sue* for Susan, but not always. For example, *Johnny* is longer than the name John. Some people use their nicknames only with family and friends. Others use their nickname most of the time. Bill Clinton is never called *William.*

TASK 1: COMPARING CUSTOMS

1. What titles are used in your culture?
2. When do people in your culture use first names? Is this common between a boss and an employee?
3. Are there nicknames in your culture? Are they just for children? Are they used only by friends and family?
4. What is the difference between Miss and Mrs.? Is it similar in the language of your culture?
5. Why do you think that some women use the title Ms. now?

TASK 2: MAKING GUESSES

*IT WORKS!
Learning Strategy:
Guessing Aids
Learning*

A. Look at the chart. Guess the full names for these common nicknames and write them down.

1. Joe	_____	**7.** Ginny	_____
2. Dot	_____	**8.** Barbie	_____
3. Tony	_____	**9.** Bob	_____
4. Chris	_____	**10.** Chuck	_____
5. Mike	_____	**11.** Jess	_____
6. Nick	_____	**12.** Dick	_____

B. What nicknames are used for these names? Can you guess?

1. Edward   _____

2. Patricia   _____

3. Ann   _____

4. Frederick_____

5. Samuel   _____

6. Jennifer   _____

TASK 3: COMMUNICATION BREAKDOWN

Read the following opinion. It is from Hans Werren, a Swiss professor working in the United States. Then write answers to the questions. Compare with your classmates.

Hans: I work in a university laboratory. The work is interesting, but I have trouble with the casual American ways. The technicians do not treat me with respect. They call me *Hans* all the time, often in front of the students. Even some students don't call me Mr. Werren, much less Doctor or Professor! I spoke up one day at a lab meeting. I explained about the importance of respect in the workplace. But nobody got the point. Afterwards, I asked another professor about it. She said, "Oh, we know you like to be formal, but we take that with a grain of salt!"

1. Why is Hans unhappy at work?

_____

2. In your opinion, what should Hans do to improve his communication with Americans?

_____

THEME 3: THE ORIGINS OF U.S. AND CANADIAN SURNAMES

Our last names come to us from our families. They are a gift from long ago. Sometimes we can learn about the past from them. We can understand traditions. The following selection, *What Is the Meaning of North American Last Names?*, tells where some common last names in Canada and the United States of America come from.

GET READY TO READ: SCAN FOR WORDS

Reading lets us see and learn new vocabulary. Scan the first and last paragraphs of the selection for these words:

First Paragraph:

1. Two other ways to say *last name:* _____ _____

2. A verb beginning with *d* that can replace *comes* in this sentence: *The word <u>comes</u> from old English.* _____.

3. A word meaning "a relative who lived long ago": _____.

4. Two words meaning "long ago": (in) _____ _____.

Last Paragraph:

1. A word meaning "people who come to live in a new country": _____.

2. A verb starting with *i* meaning "to make up (something new)": _____.

3. A word beginning with *d* that means "variety, differences": _____.

Threads

In China, the four major surnames—Li, Wang, Zhang, and Liu—are each used by more than 70 million people.

Lena H. Sun, *The Washington Post*

LEARNING STRATEGY

Forming Concepts: Thinking about the title of a reading selection before you begin prepares you to receive new facts.

GET READY TO READ:
THINKING ABOUT THE TITLE BEFORE READING

Sometimes we read to answer a question. In this case the title is a question. Before you read, think about what you already know regarding this question. That way you prepare your mind to receive new facts. Look at the common North American names below. What do you think they mean? Look at the illustration on the next page. Make a guess about each name. Then read the essay to see if you are right.

MacDonald	Robertson	Long	Baker
O'Bryan	Clark	Cooper	Hill

What is the meaning of North American last names?

by B. Dominski

Everyone in the United States and Canada has a last name (also called surname or family name). There are over one and a half million last names just in the United States.

Where do these names come from? A large number of last names come from Great Britain. They are of English, Scottish, Welsh, or Irish origin. Many derive from the occupations of ancestors, like *Carpenter, Cook, Clark* (clerk or scholar), and *Fletcher* (maker of arrows). The most common surname in North America is *Smith. Smith* derives from "blacksmith," the worker who used to make iron shoes for horses. Smiths also made swords for soldiers, and metal implements. *Cooper* means "barrel maker," important work in olden times when wooden barrels were the means of packaging.

Some family names derive from the custom of naming a man by referring to his father. *Johnson* and *Peterson* mean "son of John," "son of Peter," *Mac* and *Fitz* also mean "son of" as in *Fitzgerald* or *MacDonald*. The *O'* in many Irish surnames, like *O'Hara* or *O'Grady*, means "grandson of."

Some last names refer to a place or object near an ancestor's home, such as *Hill, Field, Church,* or *Street.* Others derive from nicknames describing personal appearance or qualities, such as *Short, Big, Smart, Strong,* or *Longfellow.*

Long ago there were no surnames. People used to talk about their neighbors. Sometimes they were confused. "Do you mean David from the river?" "No, I mean David the strong one." "Oh, David, Erick's son." "No, not David, Erick's son. David John's son!" With time the descriptions became last names: *River, Strong, Erickson, Johnson.*

The United States and Canada are countries of immigrants, so many last names are not British. Their origins are Arabic, Chinese, Fillipino, French, German, Hungarian, Indonesian, Israeli, Japanese, Polish, Serbian, Spanish, and Swiss, to name just a

few. Many of these surnames also have meanings, like the Spanish *Rodriguez* ("son of Rodrigo") and the French *Dupont,* ("from the bridge").

The ancestors of most Black Americans were brought from Africa and forced to work as slaves. They lost their African names. American slaves became free in 1863. Many chose their new names, like Jones or Lincoln. Some took African names such as *Cudjo* for a boy or *Juba* for a girl, both meaning "born on Tuesday."

Often people do not know the meaning of their names. Sometimes immigrants came to Canada and the United States, and the officials at the border could not understand their names. So they had to invent new names to put on the documents. Nowadays this seems wrong. In North America today there is more respect for the diversity of cultures.

TASK 1: CHECKING COMPREHENSION

1. What last names mean *son of* someone? *grandson of* someone?
2. What other meanings do surnames have?
3. Why did people start to use surnames?
4. When did some ancestors of Black Americans choose their names?
5. What happened at the border to the names of many immigrants in the past? What do Americans and Canadians think of this today?
6. What diverse groups of people live in your culture?

TASK 2: EXPLAINING THE MEANING OF SURNAMES

Think about what you just read about surnames. Try to explain the origins of these:

Robinson	MacGregor	Hunter	Armstrong
Martínez	Lightfoot	Stone	O'Donnell

TASK 3: MAKING A CLASS LIST OF NAMES AND MEANINGS

Write your whole name clearly and neatly in your native language. Then write it clearly and neatly in English. Afterward, write one to five sentences about your name. In your culture, is the last name written first? Do you have a nickname? Does your name have a religious meaning? Does it refer to a place, an animal, or an occupation? Were you named after a family member or a famous person? Write these or other facts about your name. Your class may decide to combine all the papers into a class name list. This can be put on the wall. Or else, take turns going to the front, writing your names on the board and telling about them.

TASK 4: A AS IN APPLE, B AS IN BOAT, SPELLING OUT YOUR NAME

The United States and Canada are countries of immigrants. Culture is diverse. There are many different names. It is often hard to understand them. A common custom is for people to spell out their name, letter by letter. To be clear, they use guide words for each letter. Read the following phone conversation.

SECRETARY Megathon Incorporated. May I help you?

CALLER Hello. Yes, I would like to speak with Mr. Howard Townsend, please.

SECRETARY Mr. Townsend is not in right now. Do you want to leave a message?

CALLER Yes, please. Tell him that Mr. Koi Phong called.

SECRETARY Excuse me?

CALLER Mr. Koi Phong.

SECRETARY Mr. Chung?

CALLER Let me spell it for you. Koi. <u>K</u> as in *Kevin,* <u>o</u> as in *old,* <u>i</u> as in *ice cream.* That's the first name. The last name is Phong. <u>P</u> as in *Peter,* <u>h</u> as in *Henry,* <u>o</u> as in *old,* <u>n</u> as in *no,* g as in *good.* Koi Phong.

SECRETARY I'll repeat. K-o-i Koi, P-h-o-n-g Phong.

CALLER That's right.

SECRETARY Very good, Mr. Phong. I'll tell Mr. Townsend you called.

CALLER Thank you. Good-bye.

SECRETARY Good-bye.

Work with a partner. Read the conversation aloud, one person as the secretary and the other as Mr. Phong. Then take turns using your own names. Spell out your name, letter by letter, using guide words. (For example, use common names like Mary or John, or names of fruits or animals.) Your partner should write down your name. Check to see that he or she has understood.

TASK 5: DESCRIBING HABITS IN THE PAST WITH THE WORDS "USED TO"

Reading brings us new ideas. Reading can also show us new language patterns. We often use *used to* + verb to describe habits in the past. These can be repeated actions or situations.

EXAMPLES: When we were young, we *used to ride* horses.

They always *used to study* together.

How many times does *used to* appear in the reading selection? Invent three sentences with *used to* by finishing the following:

1. When we were children, we . . .
2. When they were young, my parents . . .
3. Many years ago my grandparents . . .

YOUR PERSONAL JOURNAL: WRITING ABOUT YOUR CHILDHOOD

Think back to when you were a child. What people were important to you (in a good or bad way)? Make a list of the names of three people you remember well, and write about each one. Tell what they used to do and what they used to say. Tell what you used to think of them. Do you still have the same opinion of them now?

TASK 6: OUTSIDE ASSIGNMENTS

Your teacher may give you one of the following assignments or let you choose one. Work on it outside of class. To get the ball rolling, you may be given time in class to share information with two or three others. Later, your group will give a report to the class.

A. Scanning a Telephone Book
Find a telephone book of an American or Canadian city and scan for the following information. How many of these surnames can you find? Are there other interesting last names?

1. three that come from an occupation
2. three that derive from a place or object
3. three that refer to personal appearance or qualities
4. three that mean "son of" or "grandson of" someone
5. three that seem French or Spanish
6. three from your culture

B. The Names Around Us

Find out the origin, or interesting information, about the names of some of the following. Are they taken from nature? From appearance? From the names of famous people? From businesses?

1. streets, avenues, and highways
2. natural features like rivers, hills, and mountains
3. important buildings, landmarks, and parks

C. Working with a Map

Look at some maps of the United States and Canada. What regions have a lot of names that derive from French? From Spanish? From Native American cultures? Can you find out the meanings of some of these names? What cities are named for older cities in other countries? Which names are hard to pronounce for you?

THEME 4: WHEN OUR NAME BECOMES A PROBLEM

Can names be a form of oppression? Are names sometimes a block to communication, rather than a help? Let's consider the ideas of two women on the subject, a modern writer and a traditional poet.

A. Changing Customs for Women's Surnames

In the U.S.A. and Canada, most women lose their surnames. They marry and take their husband's last name. Then husband, wife, and children all have the same surname. This is not true in some other cultures. In Spain and Latin America, women keep their maiden name (the surname they have before marriage). Children use two surnames: father's and mother's. In the last few years, some North American women have begun to keep their maiden name after marriage, just as Hispanic women do. Sometimes their children use their mother's and father's surnames, often with a hyphen in between. (For example, the children of Jessica Wright and Nate Carter could use Wright-Carter as a last name.)

The following reading selection, *The Last Name Dilemma,* talks about this recent change in customs. It expresses a strong point of view about it.

**Managing Your Learning: Skimming helps you get the
main ideas or points of view.**

GET READY TO READ:
SKIMMING FOR THE POINT OF VIEW

Our *point of view* on a subject is our way of looking at it. People have
strong opinions on the subject of women's last names. Before reading the
selection, skim it to find out the author's point of view on this subject. To
skim, read the whole selection quickly. Move your eyes *back and forth*
over all the sentences. Skimming is different from scanning. You *scan* for
small bits of information, like facts or details, and stop when you find them
When you *skim,* you move through the whole reading. Don't stop at
difficult words! Skip them. Start now. When you finish, choose one of the
following:

The author . . .

a. presents both sides of the question equally. Some women should keep
their maiden names and others should take their husband's surname.
b. believes that all married women should keep their maiden names.
They should not take their husband's name.
c. thinks that all married women should take their husband's names.
They should never keep their own.

How long did it take you to find out the author's point of view? Read
the selection to understand this dilemma (difficult problem) better.

The last name dilemma

by Sharan Lebell

What's your last
name? Where did
you get it? Is it
your father's? Your
husband's? Your
former husband's?
What about having
your own? If you are a parent, what
last name do your children have?
Do you feel that you have the *right*
last name? These questions would
have seemed preposterous until recently. Not long ago, the *Bay Guard-
ian* newspaper in San Francisco
chose this as its "Ad of the Week":

Many people are rethinking the
traditional way of giving last names.

HELP US NAME THE BABY!

Dad has his name.
Mom has hers.
What do we name the baby?

What did you do?
  His?
    Hers?   Write │ **BABY**
      Hyphen?   **339 Pine Street**
                             Bigtown, ANYWHERE

  IDEAS, PLEASE.

There is growing understanding that a connection exists between how we're named and how we think of ourselves. Many married women are refusing to live in the shadow of their husbands. They no longer take their husband's last names. These women are affirming their individuality. They are keeping their birth names, just as men do. What's more, parents are questioning the custom of giving children their fathers' last names.

I'm often asked why I make such a big deal about last names. To most people, a last name is a fact. There is no choice. Yet it's clear that the way we are named and the way our children are named is unfair. Women usually lose their maiden names when they marry. Men keep their names for life and pass them on to their children. Since childhood I have been vexed by our naming customs.

I am speaking with Harry, a man who is married. His wife's maiden name is Debbie Smith. I say, "Okay, Harry, your name is now <u>Mr. Debbie Smith</u> and your children are called Debbie Smith, Jr., Robin Smith, etc.? At this point, the man laughs. The idea seems so preposterous. He cannot take the example seriously.

TASK 1: GUESSING THE MEANING

The author uses a long, somewhat unusual word two times: *preposterous.* Say the word aloud. It is stressed on the second syllable. Scan for it. It comes at the beginning and at the end. Look at the context (the words around it) and try to guess the meaning.

Choose the right meaning for *preposterous*: _____

a. wonderful and exciting
b. frightening and bad

c. completely crazy
d. rather funny

TASK 2: CHECKING COMPREHENSION

1. People put ads in the newspaper because they want something. What do the people want in the ad about the baby?
2. In the reading selection it says there is a relationship (connection) between two things. What are those two things?
3. Why don't some women take their husband's last names?
4. Why has the author been vexed (angry, upset) since childhood?
5. Who is Harry? What name does the author give him?
6. What is Harry's reaction? Is he vexed? Why or why not?

TASK 3: EXPRESSING A BRIEF OPINION

What do you think about the idea of calling Harry *Mr. Debbie Smith*? What do you think about women keeping their maiden names after marriage? Write your opinion in two or three sentences.

TASK 4: SEEING OTHER POINTS OF VIEW

IT WORKS!
Learning Strategy:
Looking for
Similarities and
Differences

If possible, sit in a circle or semi-circle with some classmates. One person gets the ball rolling by reading what he or she wrote for the exercise *Expressing a Brief Opinion.* Compare the opinions. Is there a difference between the men's and the women's opinions? Is there a difference because of age or culture? Do some people consider the ideas in this article preposterous? Do other people consider them logical? Explain.

Look back at what you wrote in your journal on *Describing the Names on Your Family Tree* (page 46). Look especially at the names of all the women: your mother, grandmother, great-grandmother, sisters, cousins, etc. What happened to their maiden names after marriage? Describe the customs for naming women in your culture. Try to imagine your mother or sister's reactions to the ideas presented in the reading. Write what you think those reactions would be.

B. The Person Behind the Name

One of the most original poems about names was written by Emily Dickinson, a famous American poet. She lived not far from Boston at Amherst, Massachusetts, from 1830–1886. Emily was not well-known during her life. In fact, some people even thought she was crazy. After her death, her fame spread throughout the whole world. All her poems are short. Some tell about nature and deep emotions, like love, sadness, grief, and wonder. Others, like this one, make fun of human actions with a gentle humor.

Emily Dickinson

Reading a poem is different from reading an article. A poem is a bit like music. The sound and emotions are as important as the ideas. To hear the sounds and feel the emotions, read the poem aloud. Do this exercise to learn about English rhyme. Then read the poem several times.

1. English poems often use *rhyme,* the matching of the end sound in two words. For example, *day* rhymes with *play.* How many other words can you think of that rhyme with *day*? Write down three:

   _____   _____   _____

2. Usually, the rhyme in English poems comes at the end of a verse (line of poetry). In this poem, which verses rhyme?

   _____

3. Sometimes a poem has a regular pattern of rhyme. Sometimes it has an irregular pattern. Sometimes there is no rhyme in the poem. Which is true of this poem?

   a. regular pattern   **b.** irregular pattern   **c.** no rhyme at all

GET READY TO READ:
THINKING ABOUT THE TITLE

Imagine you are at a party. You walk up to a woman and ask her what her name is. What do you expect her to say? Read the poem to hear a different answer.

I'm Nobody.
Who Are You?

by Emily Dickinson

I'm Nobody. Who are you?
Are you Nobody too?
Then there's a pair of us!
Don't tell. They'd banish° us—you know.   *send (us) away*

How dreary° to be Somebody.   *dull, depressing*
How public, like a frog°,   *small animal that makes*
Who tells his name the livelong day   *a croaking sound*
To an admiring bog°!   *wet, marshy place*

TASK 1: CHECKING COMPREHENSION

1. What name does the poet give?
2. Why do you think she gives that name?
3. In your opinion, who are the "they" she mentions?
4. How does she feel about them?
5. What does she think of the "Somebodies"?
6. What comparison does she make?

TASK 2: EXPRESSING YOUR OPINION

In your opinion, what is the main idea of the poem? Write a comment about it in two to five sentences. Compare with your classmates.

LOOKING BACK ON CHAPTER 3

Take a moment to look back at the goals for this chapter. What ideas and skills did you learn? How many pages did you write in your Personal Journal? Your teacher can help you measure your progress. But you must learn for yourself. The following exercises can serve as a review of some of the key vocabulary from the chapter. (Answers are given in the Answer Appendix at the end of the book.)

VOCABULARY REVIEW: SYNONYMS AND SHORT DEFINITIONS

Match each word in the first column to the correct synonym or short definition in the second column.

1. _____ advice	**a.** look through quickly for ideas	
2. _____ ancestor	**b.** custom	
3. _____ casual	**c.** totally crazy	
4. _____ diverse	**d.** work	
5. _____ dilemma	**e.** look through quickly for details	
6. _____ immigrant	**f.** varied	
7. _____ occupation	**g.** relative from the past	
8. _____ preposterous	**h.** rhyme	
9. _____ pronounce	**i.** last name	
10. _____ scan	**j.** person coming to a new place	
11. _____ skim	**k.** say out loud	
12. _____ surname	**l.** informal	
	m. suggestion	
	n. problem	

VOCABULARY REVIEW: WORD FAMILIES

Fill in the missing members of the word families. The first one is done for you.

VERB	-*ING* FORM	NOUN.
1. repeat	repeating	repetition
2. explain	_____	_____
3. _____	introducing	_____
4. _____	_____	description
5. pronounce	_____	_____
6. _____	informing	_____
7. _____	_____	assignment
8. _____	suggesting	_____
9. _____	_____	agreement

Why Do Some Foods Taste So Good?

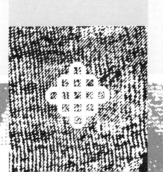

INTRODUCTION

All people must eat to survive. But what they eat, when they eat, and the way they eat are patterned to a great extent by their culture. Certain foods are staples (necessary items); others are delicacies (special treats). A food considered a delicacy in one society can cause a person in a different society to feel ill. A Moslem might feel this way about eating pork, an American or Canadian about eating horse meat, and a vegetarian from India about eating *any* kind of meat. Where, when, what, and how people eat are interesting points of observation for someone visiting a new society. In this chapter we will explore some North American eating habits and compare and contrast them with those of other cultures.

Think about some goals for your own improvement.

To learn more about:

- Good tastes and bad tastes
- What North Americans eat and drink
- Where and when meals are eaten
- Hidden similarities among many different eating customs
- Some ways of being polite while eating

To practice skills:

- Interviewing and being interviewed
- Observing and comparing language and customs
- Describing past experiences
- Identifying the main idea of a reading
- Speaking and listening in a group
- Defending an opinion

To acquire new vocabulary

THEME 1: *GOOD* AND *BAD* ARE RELATIVE WORDS FOR TASTE

What makes something taste good or bad? Almost everyone remembers the experience of trying a new food. You taste it and find it delicious, or disgusting, or somewhere in between. But a friend may try the same food and have a very different opinion. So, who is right and who is wrong? Nobody. Taste is relative. It depends on culture and individual preference.

64

A. The Many Attitudes Toward Meat

A clear example of the relativity of taste is the many different attitudes toward eating meat. Some people do not eat any meat; they are called vegetarians. In most cultures, some kinds of meat are eaten and others are taboo (forbidden). Most Americans and Canadians are carnivores (meat eaters), but they do not eat all kinds of meat. Are you a carnivore? Look at the chart called *Animals As Food,* and work out the exercises that follow it. All the animals shown are eaten in some part of the world.

TASK 1: MATCHING

Match the number of the correct picture from the chart to each name on the list below.

LIST OF NAMES

dog	deer	fish	lobster
buffalo	pig	ant	octopus
horse	snake	goat	frog
cow	rabbit	chicken	sheep

TASK 2: TALKING IT OVER

1. Which of the animals do you think of as food?
2. Which do you like? Which would you never eat?
3. Which are delicacies in some societies? Which are taboo?
4. Seven of these animals are not usually eaten in Canada or the United States. Can you guess which ones they are?
5. In some cases, a different word is used to refer to an animal as food. In Spanish, for example, *pez* refers to a living fish and *pescado* to fish served as food. In English, what words are used for *cow, pig,* and *sheep* when served as food?
6. In your opinion, why are some animals *not* used as food?

TASK 3: DESCRIBING A FAVORITE FOOD

Think of something you like to eat. It can be a fruit or vegetable or a complete dish. Draw a picture of it and write its name in your native language. (Don't worry if your picture is not a piece of art. It is only an aid for your explanation.) Show it to the class or to a small group. Tell some facts about it. Find out how many of your classmates have eaten this food.

LEARNING STRATEGY

Managing Your Learning: Interviewing others and being interviewed develops social skills and conversational fluency.

TASK 4: INTERVIEWING A CLASSMATE ABOUT ACQUIRED TASTES

Just like meat, fruit can provoke strong reactions. Have you ever heard of the *durian*? Many Chinese and Malaysians love it, but not usually when they take the first bite. According to a Chinese saying, *The durian tastes like heaven, smells like hell!* It smells so bad that most people don't want to try it. But once they get used to it, they are crazy about it and sometimes pay very high prices for it. North Americans would call the taste for this fruit an *acquired taste* because it takes time to get used to. Foods like artichokes and avocados or drinks like coffee or scotch whiskey are usually considered acquired tastes. Interview a classmate on this topic.

How to Conduct an Interview

First, introduce yourself and find out the name of the person you are interviewing. Then ask him or her the interview questions, one at a time. Take notes about the most interesting details, but don't try to write down everything. Then let your partner interview you. When being interviewed, speak slowly and clearly. If there is a question you don't want to answer, simply say, "I don't know about that. Let's go to the next question." After you both finish, write a few sentences about the tastes of the person you interviewed.

Interview Questions

1. Have you ever tasted a durian? If not, would you like to?
2. What about an artichoke or an avocado? Would you try them?
3. Do you drink coffee or scotch? Why or why not?
4. What foods or drinks from your culture need an acquired taste?
5. What is the most unusual food you have ever eaten? How did you feel afterwards?
6. What new foods or drinks have you sampled recently? What new foods do you want to try?
7. (Add your own question here.) _____

_____

YOUR PERSONAL JOURNAL: DESCRIBING AN EATING EXPERIENCE

Write about a pleasant or unpleasant experience with food. Tell where and when it happened and what people you were with. Was it a special occasion or just an everyday meal? Describe how the food looked, how it smelled and tasted. How did you feel? Happy? Relaxed? Upset? Confused? Tell about your feelings and why you felt that way.

B. Food Staples in Different Cultures

Each culture has its own cuisine* (style of cooking), and each cuisine depends on certain staples. Staples are the foods that you always keep in your kitchen and use almost every day. They are the foods you can't do without. The following foods are staples in at least one culture around the world. Read the list and try to picture each item in your mind.

bananas	corn	milk	rice
beans	eggs	mustard	salad dressing
bread	flour	noodles	salt
butter	ketchup	oil	soy sauce
cabbage	lemons	pasta	sugar
cheese	lettuce	pepper	tea
chocolate	margarine	potatoes	tofu
coffee	mayonnaise		

_____
*The word *cuisine* is of French origin. It is pronounced *kwee ZEEN.*

Threads

—There is no accounting for taste.

—You are what you eat.

—One man's meat is another man's poison.

English proverbs

IT WORKS!
Learning Strategy:
Describing Your
Emotions

TASK 1: TALKING IT OVER

1. Which items from the list are staples in your culture?
2. Are there other staples that should be added to the list?
3. Which staples do you think are used most in North America?

TASK 2: WORKING WITH "WHATCHA-MA-CALLIT"

Some kinds of bananas are eaten raw. In some cultures, other kinds of bananas are cooked: fried, roasted, or baked. Choose one of the staples above and describe how you use it to prepare food. But don't say the name of the food. Say the slang word *whatcha-ma-callit* instead. (If you can't pronounce it, say *thinga-ma-jig.* These are slang words people use when they can't remember the names of things.) See how long it takes before someone can guess what staple you're talking about !

> **EXAMPLE:** I mix *whatcha-ma-callit* with eggs. Then I put in butter. I use this to make a cake. (flour)

THEME 2: THE GREAT DIVERSITY OF FOODS IN NORTH AMERICA

Visitors from other lands are often amazed at the variety of foods in American or Canadian supermarkets. There are many kinds of fruits and vegetables, a large number of different meats and fish, a big selection of frozen and packaged items. Why do Americans and Canadians eat so many different kinds of foods? Try to think of three reasons and write them down now.

1. _____
2. _____
3. _____

A. The Truth About American (and Canadian) Cooking

The reading selection, *How to Cook Like an American,* comes from *Gourmet* magazine. It deals with one important reason for the great diversity of foods in North America. Read the article and see if the reason it talks about is on your list.

GET READY TO READ:
GUESSING THE MEANING OF IDIOMS

THEME 2:
THE GREAT DIVERSITY OF
FOODS IN
NORTH AMERICA

Guessing the Meaning of Three New Idioms

Here are three idioms from the article *How to Cook Like an American,* with illustrations of what the words say. Guess what each idiom means. If necessary, scan the article and look at the idioms in context.

*IT WORKS!
Learning Strategy:
Guessing New
Expressions*

1. to eat like a horse

2. to draw a blank

**3. to turn the tables
on someone**

How to Cook Like an American

by Laurie Colwin

There is nothing like a visitor from another continent to confuse you about your own homeland. One night an Indian friend came to dinner. He was a pleasure to feed because he was skinny and ate like a horse. I cooked him an Indian dish and then asked him questions about the ingredients and presentation of the meal. After the meal he turned the tables on me.

He asked me to help him figure out American cooking. At this point I drew a blank. He said: I would like to cook some American dishes, but it is hard for me to tell just what American food is.

Of course it was doubly hard for him because he lives in New York City, where *hummus, sushi, bagels,* and *jerk chicken* are all considered standard foods.

I tried to put together an imaginary sample meal for my Indian friend: fried chicken (which the Chinese have been cooking for thousands of years), gumbo (of African origin) and coleslaw (from Germany). And for dessert, there would be strawberry shortcake, which is like an English shortbread or biscuit. No wonder he was confused! I was pretty confused myself.

—Gourmet

TASK 1: TALKING IT OVER

1. Who came to dinner at the writer's home?
2. Why was he "a pleasure to feed"?
3. What kind of food was served?
4. What questions did the writer ask his guest?
5. How did his guest turn the tables on him?
6. Are hummus, sushi, bagels, and jerk chicken considered standard or foreign in New York City? Why?
7. Do you know what cultures these foods are from? Have you tasted them? Have you tasted other ethnic foods, like egg rolls or tacos?
8. Why did the guest and the writer feel confused?

TASK 2: CHOOSING THE CORRECT MEANING

Select the correct meaning for each idiom.

1. *to eat like a horse*
   a. to be sloppy and rude while eating
   b. to eat a lot
   c. to eat in a courteous way
2. *to draw a blank*
   a. to become upset by someone's words
   b. to be surprised
   c. to be unable to think of an answer
3. *to turn the tables (on someone)*
   a. to reverse or completely change a situation for another person
   b. to knock the table over so that the food goes on the floor
   c. to change the subject of a conversation in an abrupt manner

TASK 3: STATING THE MAIN IDEA

Write a sentence of your own stating the main idea of the article. Get right to the point and tell what it was about.

_____

_____

_____

_____

B. Selecting and Buying Foods

Look at the pictures below. Which one looks most like a shopping scene from your culture? Why? What place do you like to shop at?

TASK 1: COMPLETING A DESCRIPTION

Complete the following description by choosing the best phrases. Share your descriptions with your classmates.

SHOPPING IN MY CULTURE

The photo that shows _____ is most like shopping in my culture.

In (name of your country or culture: _____), the ones who select and buy foods are usually (the husbands, the wives, the children, other relatives, servants). The place for food shopping is _____. It is generally done (every day, on Saturday morning, on Sundays, in the evenings, _____). Most people think of it as (a terrible job, just another chore, often enjoyable, _____). When I am living at home, I myself (often, sometimes, rarely, never) do the shopping. The biggest difference I see between food in my culture and food in North America is _____.

Shopping for foods in North America

Warehouse Supermarket

Open-air Market

Convenience Store

Neighborhood Grocery

Remembering New Material: Word association, such as rhyme, helps you remember new vocabulary.

TASK 2: RHYME TIME WITH NAMES OF FRUITS

How many names of fruits can you think of in English? Fill in the nonsense rhymes with the correct names. Each name rhymes with the word in italics. More than one answer is sometimes possible.

1. If you're hungry, *reach* for a _____ peach _____.

2. Some folks like to dance a *tango,* others like to eat a _____.

3. Don't feel *glum;* just eat a _____.

4. A cowboy can wear a *bandana* and eat a _____.

5. It's nice to *share* a green or yellow _____.

6. It would be hard to *grapple* with a twenty-pound _____.

7. It isn't *scary* to eat a _____.

8. People, monkeys, and *apes* like to eat _____.

YOUR PERSONAL JOURNAL: WRITING THE SCRIPT

Work alone or with a partner. Choose one of the photos of stores on page 72. Write down what you think two people shopping at that store might be saying. Put your writing in dialogue form. (Use quotation marks for the exact words people say. See page 29 to review use of quotation marks.) If you want, invent names for the people, or call them by descriptive terms, *first boy, second boy, man in white shirt, woman with bag,* etc. Your teacher may ask you to select a part of your script to share with the class.

TASK 3: OUTSIDE ASSIGNMENTS

Your teacher may give you one of the following assignments or let you choose one. Work outside of class. You may get time in class to share information with others who are working on the same assignment. Then, alone or with others, make a report to your teacher and classmates. They may ask you questions, so be sure to prepare well.

A. Coupons, Coupons, Coupons

Get a Sunday newspaper (or the newspaper with the most coupons). Look over the food ads and choose some of the best ones. Show them to the class and explain why they are good and how to use them. Find coupons for some staples and for some luxuries (special things we don't really need).

B. Expert on Vegetables

Go to the produce department in a supermarket with a notebook. Write down the names of all the different vegetables you can find. After each one, draw a picture of its shape and describe its color and general appearance. Tell the class about them. Draw the unusual ones on the board, or show your pictures or drawings.

C. Expert on Fruits

Follow the directions for assignment B, but use fruits instead of vegetables.

D. Price Detective

Visit three stores (of different kinds, if possible, such as a convenience store, a warehouse supermarket, and a specialty store). Find the prices for the items listed in the price comparison table that follows. (Be sure to give the unit price.) Share your data with the class and give them your opinion on the general quality of the store. Tell them which store you would choose and why.

Price Comparison Table

	STORE 1	STORE 2	STORE 3
Name of Store			
Type of Store			
1. one gallon of milk			
2. five lbs. of sugar			
3. one loaf of white bread			
4. laundry detergent			
5. toothpaste			

THEME 3: WHERE, WHEN, AND HOW WE EAT: SIMILARITIES AND DIFFERENCES

There are many differences among cultures. Most of these are on the surface. Underneath the differences we usually find that people have similar needs, desires, and feelings. Let's examine some eating customs and look for the similarities that underlie the differences.

A. Eating At Home

In your culture, how many meals are there each day? When are they served? In North America, there are typically three meals each day: breakfast, lunch, and the evening meal called supper or dinner.

In some European countries, such as France and Spain, the main meal is in the middle of the day, at around 2 P.M. Businesses and schools take a two- or three-hour break. Most people come home to eat with their families. Then they return to work or school. This means that there are four rush hours (times of heavy traffic) each day.

The chart that follows gives the typical meal schedule* for Americans and Canadians. Look at the chart and answer the questions.

*Canadians and Americans pronounce the word *schedule* differently. Canadians (and people from England) say *SHED yool.* Americans say *SKEJ ool.* However, the word has the same meaning: a timetable or list of times of recurring events, such as a schedule for trains, meals or classes.

Typical Meal Schedule in North America

MEAL	STARTING TIME	PLACE	WHAT IS SERVED
breakfast	6–8 A.M.	home	juice, tea, or coffee cereal or toast sometimes eggs and bacon, ham, or sausages
lunch	12–1 P.M.	work or home	sandwiches and fruit or soup and salad
supper (dinner)	5:30–7:00 P.M.	home	meat or fish, potatoes, pasta or rice, two vegeta- bles or one vegetable and one salad and dessert
snack	anytime	any place	cheese and crackers, pretzels, potato chips, ice cream or fruit

TASK 1: TALKING IT OVER

1. Which meal do you think is the main meal for most North Americans? At what time is it served?

2. What time is the main meal served in your culture? Is the serving time more similar to the main meal in Spain and France or to the main meal in North America?

3. Why do you think the main meal is served at different times in different cultures?

4. Sometimes on weekends or holidays Americans and Canadians invite friends over for *brunch*. What do you think *brunch* is?

TASK 2: READING FOR SPECIFIC INFORMATION

The following short selection is from a cookbook written by a group of Polish-American housewives in Minneapolis, Minnesota. Read the selection to find out what the meal schedule is like in Poland.

Eating Time in Poland

by the Polanie Club of Minneapolis

In the cities, the average working hours are from seven in the morning to three-thirty in the afternoon. Breakfast is served at six-thirty, lunch, *drugie 'sniadanie,* at eleven o'clock, dinner at three-thirty or four in the afternoon, and supper at seven-thirty in the evening. The main meal is supper. On the farms, the tillers of the soil eat their breakfast at sunrise, pack a lunch and eat in the field when they get hungry and return to their homes at sunset for supper.

A delightful Polish custom is the break in the afternoon routine for a visit to the many tea shops. This is done between the hours of three and six o'clock in the afternoon. The pastries in the tea shop offer you an amazing array of choices. You may order a piece of cake, a cream puff, or any of the many other delicacies.

Threads

—A good appetite needs no sauce.

—Without work there is no bread.

Polish proverbs

TASK 3: FILLING IN A CHART TO SHOW COMPARISON AND CONTRAST

Fill in the following chart. Compare answers with your classmates.

MEAL SCHEDULES IN THREE CULTURES

	POLAND (CITY PEOPLE)	NORTH AMERICA	YOUR CULTURE
Number of meals			
Time of breakfast			
Time of second meal			
Time of last meal			
Time of other meal(s) or snack(s)			
When the main meal is served			

IT WORKS! Learning Strategy: Looking for Similarities and Differences

TASK 4: MAKING COMPARISONS

1. What differences in eating customs are there between city people and country people in Poland? Are there differences between city and country people in your culture too? Explain.
2. What differences between cultures do you see on your chart?
3. What similarities are there?
4. In your culture, who is present at the main meal? What is served? Is this the same as it was ten years ago? Or has it changed?

TASK 5: DEFENDING AN OPINION

What is the best schedule for meals? Just for the sake of argument, complete this sentence, choosing one culture. Then list some advantages of that schedule over other schedules.

The best meal schedule is the (North American, Bolivian, Vietnamese, Polish, etc.) because:

1. _____,

2. _____,

3. _____.

Read and compare opinions with your classmates. Does everybody agree? Did everyone choose his or her own culture? Is one way better than another, or does it depend on circumstances?

B. Eating Out

Threads

One-fifth of Americans eat in a fast food restaurant each day.

Thirty out of 100 Americans go out for dinner once a week. There is an amazing diversity of restaurants in North America. Choices are French, Mexican, Thai, Greek, Chinese, Japanese, Slavic, Italian, Spanish, African, and Arabic, among others. These are called ethnic restaurants because they serve food from other cultures. Traditional North American restaurants are also popular, serving typical dishes like steak, potatoes, and salad. Then, of course, there are those *very* North American institutions: take-outs, cafeterias, and drive-ins.

In some restaurants, you use utensils—forks, knives, spoons, or even chopsticks (for Chinese or Japanese food). In others, you eat with your hands. You serve yourself in some restaurants, and in others there are four waiters to serve your table. Although some restaurants in the United States and Canada require a tie and jacket for men and formal dress for women, most are informal.

Let's read a true story that happened in one of the most popular kinds of restaurants in North America.

TASK 1: USING THE TITLE TO PREDICT THE SUBJECT OF A READING

The following reading is a true story written by a woman from Korea who studied in Madison, Wisconsin, in the United States. Look at the title. What do you understand by the word *embarrassing*? Write what you think the story will be about.

_____

_____

*IT WORKS!
Learning Strategy:
Using the Title to
Predict the Subject*

Read the selection to see if you are right.

A most embarrassing moment

by Soon Hee Park

When we first came to the United States, my husband and I saw a restaurant called Pizza Hut. We had never heard of pizza, but we went in anyway. With the two children, Brian who was three, and Doug who was one year old, we chose a table in the middle of the room and sat down.

The waitress came to us and said, "May I help you?"

My husband answered, "Yes, please, pizza for the four of us, but I don't know what pizza is."

She pointed to the table nearest us and said, "They are having pizza. It's a combination of meat, cheese, and tomato baked on bread."

My husband said, "We'll have four pizzas—a large one for me, a large one for my wife, a medium one for Brian, and a small one for the baby."

With surprise on her face and suppressed laughter, the waitress said, "Are you sure you can eat all that?" My husband said, "Of course. Don't worry."

When the pizza finally came, what a shock we got! The customers all looked at us and at each other with knowing glances wondering what we would do with all that pizza. Of course, we ate some of the pizza and, I might say, found it to be very tasty. The waitress came up to us and said, "Is everything all right?"

"Just fine," my husband said, "but we ordered too much food."

Smiling, she said, "Would you like a container to carry home the extra pizza?" We were so embarrassed! Needless to say, we had pizza for days. Believe me, we avoided Pizza Hut for a long time afterward.

TASK 2: TALKING IT OVER

1. Who went into the Pizza Hut? Describe each person.
2. How did the waitress explain pizza to the family?
3. What did the husband order?
4. What mistake did he make?
5. Do you know what a *doggie bag* is? Would you use one? What do you think of this custom?
6. Did the waitress give enough information? Explain.
7. Why was the visit to the pizza place so embarrassing?
8. Have you ever had a funny experience with food? Can you describe what happened?

YOUR PERSONAL JOURNAL: DESCRIBING AN EMBARRASSING MOMENT

Think about some time when you felt embarrassed. Tell where you were, who was with you, and what happened. Describe how you felt then and how you feel about it now.

TASK 3: OUTSIDE ASSIGNMENT: INTERVIEWING OTHERS

Interview three Americans or Canadians about their restaurant habits. How often do they go out to eat? Where? For what meal? (breakfast, supper, tea time, etc.?) Fill in the chart below for each person. Then interview three international students about restaurant habits in their native countries. Be careful! The people you interview may turn the tables on you and ask about *your* restaurant habits.

	WHAT MEAL?	DAILY	WEEKLY	MONTHLY
1. Fast food	_____	_____	_____	_____
2. Sit-down/ inexpensive	_____	_____	_____	_____
3. Sit-down/ expensive	_____	_____	_____	_____
4. Other type	_____	_____	_____	_____

TASK 4: GUESS THE ORIGIN

Pizza is a popular dish of Italian origin that has almost become a North American staple. Many ethnic dishes have entered the diet of Americans and Canadians. Can you guess the country that these foods originally came from?

sauerkraut	spaghetti	kim chee
empanadas	tempura	goulash
wonton soup	croissants	burritos

TASK 5: CHOOSING FROM A MENU

Look at the menu on the next page. It is from the University of Wisconsin cafeteria. Working in a group, make a list of the dishes that seem ethnic and try to guess their countries of origin (where they come from). Then choose one week and decide what you would order each day.

Spring 1993

Main Entree Menu
in the

LAKEFRONT CAFETERIA
Memorial Union

WEEK 1

Jan. 25-29   March 29-Apr. 2
Feb. 15-19   April 19-23
March 8-12   May 10-14

MONDAY	TUESDAY	WEDNESDAY	THURSDAY	FRIDAY

LUNCH

MONDAY		TUESDAY		WEDNESDAY		THURSDAY		FRIDAY	
Ital. Spinach Bake (v)	$1.65	Southwestern Lentils (v)	$1.79	Zucchini Casserole (v)	$1.79	Spinach Pot. Pie (v)	$2.09	Red Beans & Rice (v)	$1.79
Taco Casserole	2.24	Esc. Ham & Potatoes	1.65	Turkey & Dressing	2.09	BBQ Chicken	2.09	Lasagna	2.64
Fish Sandwich	1.94	Chicken Sandwich	2.89	BBQ Beef Sandwich	2.24	Reuben	2.48	Roast Pork Sandwich	2.44
Turkey Sub		Beef Sub		Cheese Sub		Ham & Cheese Sub		Combo Sub	
Soup: Chicken Rice		Soup: Tomato Barley		Soup: Bolivian Garbanzo Bean		Soup: Lentil		Soup: Clam Chowder	

DINNER

MONDAY		TUESDAY		WEDNESDAY		THURSDAY		FRIDAY	
Swiss Mush Quiche (v)	$1.89	Ital. Potato/Cheese (v)	$1.69	Pasta Primavera (v)	$1.94	Broc. Cheese Bake (v)	$1.74	Spag./Marinara (v)	$1.74
Tuna Tetrazzini	1.94	Chicken Tarragon	2.09	Enchilada Casserole	2.29	Roast Beef	2.04	Chix Broc. Rice Cass.	2.09
Italian Beef Ragout	2.34	Pork Chop Suey	2.19	Chicken/Wild Rice	1.94	Pork Swed. Casserole	1.79		

Daily Special: Soup & Sub Sandwich $2.95

A large variety of salads, vegetables, beverages, and desserts also available.

Lunch 11am – 3 pm
Dinner 4:45 – 6:30 pm

(v) = vegetarian

Menu items subject to change

LAKEFRONT CAFETERIA • Memorial Union

WEEK 2

Feb. 1-5   April 5-9
Feb. 22-26   April 26-30
March 15-19   May 17-21

MONDAY	TUESDAY	WEDNESDAY	THURSDAY	FRIDAY

LUNCH

MONDAY		TUESDAY		WEDNESDAY		THURSDAY		FRIDAY	
Quiche Diane (v)	$1.89	Vegetarian Pizza (v)	$1.84	Veg. Chop Suey (v)	$1.94	Tortellini (v)	$2.09	Fettucini Alfredo (v)	$1.84
Beef Stew	2.29	Walnut Chicken	2.09	Pork Mostaciolli	1.94	Chicken Enchilada Cass.	2.29	Roast Beef	2.04
BLT Sandwich	1.99	BBQ Pork Sandwich	2.24	Turkey Sandwich	2.09	Ital. Burger	1.94	Fish Sandwich	1.94
Cheese Sub		Ital. Beef Sub		Ham & Cheese Sub		Beef Sub		Turkey Sub	
Soup: Cream of Broccoli		Soup: Navy Bean		Soup: Mushroom Barley		Soup: Vegetable		Soup: Clam Chowder	

DINNER

MONDAY		TUESDAY		WEDNESDAY		THURSDAY		FRIDAY	
Mid East Lentils (v)	$1.79	Broc. Mush. Cass. (v)	$1.79	Noodles Romanoff (v)	$1.84	Pizza Rustica (v)	$1.89	Ratatouille (v)	$2.04
Salisbury Steak	1.75	Chicken Spin. Lasagna	2.29	Parmesan Chicken	2.09	Singapore Ham & Rice	1.65	Beef Chop Suey	2.19
Chicken Alfredo	1.94	German Roast Pork	2.44	Beef Empanada Pie	2.29	Beef Stroganoff	2.44		

TASK 6: OBSERVATION TOURS

Go on an observation tour with some members of your class to observe eating customs. Decide in advance where you will go and what you will look for. You can go to a special kind of restaurant, a shopping mall, a park where people are picnicking, the school cafeteria, etc. Before leaving, make up a list of guide questions for your group. (Examples: Who eats together—families, co-workers, groups of the same age? Who eats what? Where and how do they sit? How much talking is there? Who talks to whom? What are they wearing? And so on . . .)

THEME 4: WORDS AND RITUALS INVOLVING FOODS

Everybody has trouble knowing what to say and do in certain situations, especially in a different culture. Each culture has its own ways of polite speaking and special rituals involving foods and drink. Learning about them can give us confidence in social situations.

A. What We Say and Don't Say Around Food and Drink

Threads

—God helps those who help themselves!

—The doors of courtesy have two keys. One is thank you, the other is please.

Popular North American sayings

Edward T. Hall, an expert on language and culture, says that many visitors have misunderstandings in North America because they come from high-context cultures. In high-context cultures, most information is understood from the *context,* the way people look and act and the traditions and customs. It is not necessary to give much information in direct words. For example, if a person says, "This is a difficult situation for me," everyone understands that the person is angry. He or she does not need to say, "I am angry about this." In many high-context cultures it would be rude to speak so plainly.

Canada is a low-context culture and the United States even more so. In low-context cultures, most information is contained in the words people speak, not in the context. That means that Americans and Canadians often express needs and wishes directly, in plain words. To people from high-context cultures, this can seem like bad manners.

Of course, some cultures, such as the Scandanavian and Swiss German, are even more low-context than the North American. But most are more high-context. The general rule in North America, then, is: *be direct.* If you want or need something, *speak up.* Of course, you should be polite. Using *please* and *thank you* is very important in North America. The words *would* and *could* also add to politeness.

TASK 1: GUESSING THE SITUATION

Look at the list of polite phrases and try to guess the situation for each.

Some Polite Phrases Involving Food
When and why would you use them?

1. How delicious!
2. Would you like some more lasagna?
3. No, thank you. I'm full. But it was very tasty.
4. Please pass the _____ (rice, salt, or whatever).
5. I'm sorry I can't eat a lot today. I don't have much of an appetite.
6. Could I have a smaller portion (or piece), please?
7. Excuse me. Could you please tell me how to eat this?
8. Yes, please. I would like some more.
9. I really have to go now. Thank you for the wonderful dinner.

TASK 2: ACCEPTING OR REFUSING FOODS

Sit in a circle. Take a moment to think of a food or beverage to offer your neighbor. Choose one person to start. Offer your food or beverage to the classmate on your right: *Would you like to try some . . . ?* or *How about some more . . . ?* Your classmate should accept or refuse—politely—then turn to the next person. . . .

LEARNING STRATEGY

Managing Your Learning: Listening and talking in a group can develop skills that are useful in many jobs and social situations.

TASK 3: COMMUNICATION BREAKDOWN

Work in a group of three to four people to solve this problem: What caused the breakdown in communication? First, take turns reading aloud, one sentence each, of the following situation. Then give ideas about what went wrong. Be sure to listen to the ideas of the others too.* One person should write down the ideas of the group and read them to the class.

WHAT YOU DON'T SAY IN SOME NATIVE CULTURES

A Native Canadian from Southern Alberta was hitchhiking home after working down in Colorado. He didn't have any money for food and was very hungry. A car picked him up. The four people inside were eating Kentucky Fried Chicken. One of them said to him, "Are you hungry?" Another asked him, "Want some chicken?" He shook his head. Even as a little boy, he knew that you never tell people you are hungry or want to eat. If people want to share food, they give it to you. Nobody gave him any food during the four hours in the car. He almost fainted with hunger and felt sick afterwards.

---

*You may want to look over the section on How to Participate in Group Discussions in the Preface.

TASK 4: WHAT'S THE QUESTION?

Write down two questions about food or eating and drinking that you want your teacher to answer. Put them in the question box or give them to your teacher.

B. Some Rituals For Eating and Drinking

Every culture has certain rituals involving eating and drinking. Rituals are ceremonies or sets of actions we do in special circumstances. At North American weddings, for example, people throw rice at the bride and groom to wish them prosperity. At the reception, friends give speeches, often humorous ones. Then *toasts* are made to the bride and groom and their parents. To make a toast, someone raises a glass in the air and expresses a wish. At that moment, the other guests raise their glasses too and take a sip. That means they join in the wish. Another wedding ritual is the clinking of the glasses. The guests hit their glasses every once in a while with their spoons. Can you guess what the bride and groom are supposed to do when this happens?

Think about your own culture. Write a brief description of a ritual from your culture, involving food and drink.

_____

_____

_____

_____

Compare descriptions with your classmates.

TASK 1: OUTSIDE ASSIGNMENT AT THE LIBRARY: LEARNING ABOUT CUSTOMS

Go to the library and find information about one of the following special foods, eating rituals, or customs. If you prefer, find someone to interview who knows about one of these subjects. Share your information with the class.

1. Breaking plates in Greek restaurants
2. Buffet dinners
3. BYO parties
4. Cappuccino coffee and café latté
5. Cheese or beef fondue
6. Chinese tea ceremony
7. Hors d'oeurves
8. Hot pots
9. Japanese tea or saki ceremonies
10. Octoberfest
11. Paella
12. Potluck dinners
13. Roasting marshmallows
14. Sangría
15. Setting the North American table
16. Smorgasboard
17. TV dinners
18. Winetasting
19. *Yerba mate* drinking in Argentina, Brazil, and Paraguay

The Japanese Tea Ceremony (*Cha-No-Yu*) is a beautiful ritual surrounding the drinking of green tea.

TASK 2: COMPARING TABLE MANNERS

Think back to when you were a child. What did your parents tell you about how *not* to eat. In North America, parents usually say, "Don't slurp your soup," "Don't speak with your mouth full," and "Don't put your elbows on the table." Yet in some cultures these actions are not considered bad, but other ones are. Work with two or three others and make a list of things not to do at the table in your culture(s). Compare your list with the other groups.

TASK 3: COMPARING BODY LANGUAGE ACROSS CULTURES

Read the Communication Without Words box. Then answer the questions that follow.

Communication Without Words: Asking for Another Drink

How do you signal to a waiter that you want another coffee, soda, or beer? It depends on where you are.

In Canada or the United States, you hold up your index finger. If you hold up two, three, or four fingers, you will probably get that number of drinks. You do not hold up your thumb.

In Germany, you hold up your thumb. That means one. The thumb and index finger means two, and so on with the other fingers up to five.

In Japan, you hold up your index finger to ask for one drink. Holding up your thumb would mean *five* more drinks because the Japanese begin to count with the index finger and finish on the thumb.

---

1. Imagine that you are in a bar. You hold up your thumb. How many drinks would you get in Germany? In Japan?
2. If you hold up your index finger, how many drinks would you get in Canada or the United States? In Japan? In Germany?
3. How do you signal for one drink in your culture?
4. Where do you start when you count on your fingers?
5. In your culture, how do you call a waiter or waitress? North Americans usually try to "catch the waiter's eye" by waving one hand. Sometimes they call out "Waiter!" or "Waitress!", but not in a loud voice. Would these actions be considered rude in your culture?

TASK 4: GET READY TO READ: ANTICIPATING THE SUBJECT OF A READING

"American coffee," a thin, watery, black liquid, has long been a staple in Canada and the United States. Nowadays, however, a variety of coffees have become popular in North America—cappuccino, latté, espresso, café au lait. Along with these new types of coffee, Americans and Canadians have re-adopted the idea of the cafe or coffeehouse.

The following selection is from a pamphlet about coffee, called *Romancing the Bean.* Try to anticipate (see in your mind ahead of time) what you will read. Look at the title of the selection and skim the first three paragraphs. Which of the following do you expect to find in the article?

_____ statistics on the number of people drinking new types of coffee in different North American cities

_____ facts about the various uses and preparations of coffee in different cultures throughout history

_____ comparisons of the different economies in the world that depend on the production and sales of coffee

Read the article to see if you have chosen correctly and to find out more about one of the world's most popular drinks.

The origins of coffee

by Mark Ballering

The coffee plant is thought to have originated in Africa. African tribesmen used to crush coffee beans and mix them with animal fat. They would carry these nuggets of coffee with them to battle. Popping the nuggets in their mouths, they would get a quick burst of energy from the caffeine in the coffee.

Also, from Arabia, we hear early tales of goats and goatherders "getting high" on the red coffee beans in their fields. A holy man observed these rituals and brought the special beans to his monastery. The beans were then passed on from monastery to monastery in the Arabian Peninsula.

Around 1000 A.D., the Arabs learned to boil the coffee beans with water. They made a hot drink that pleased many who drank it.

In time, seeds from the coffee tree were transported to India. The Italians, English, Dutch, and French, who traded in this area, spread the coffee bean and its delights to Europe and Java.

In 1669, France's Louis XIV added a coffee tree to his luxuries. From this tree, arabica coffee beans were sent all over the world, and especially to Central and South America.

It was probably Captain John Smith who introduced coffee to the American colonies in Virginia in 1607. From the notes of William Penn, father of Pennsylvania, we see that coffee was an expensive commodity even then. He paid $4.65 per pound for beans for his black brew.

The coffeehouses of coffee's golden age (1670–1870) were centers for the common man to discuss revolutionary ideas and democracy. Often the revolutionaries who plotted in the cafes of Paris and America became the heads of their new governments.

Romancing the Bean

TASK 5: CHECKING COMPREHENSION

1. Where did coffee plants probably originate?
2. How did tribesmen there use them?
3. How were they used long ago in Arabia?
4. Who learned to boil the coffee beans about a thousand years ago?
5. Where was the coffee tree transported after that?
6. When was it brought to the American colonies?
7. Why were the coffeehouses of Paris and America important in the 1700s and 1800s?
8. How popular is coffee in your culture?
9. What other beverages do people in your culture drink often?

TASK 6: SCANNING FOR VOCABULARY

Scan the reading selection for the words or phrases that correspond to the following meanings. They are in the order of their appearance.

1. small round units (of gold, coffee or something else): *n*_____

2. a two-word phrase meaning *entering into an excited or altered state of mind:* g_____ *h*_____

3. to carry or move from one place to another: t_____

4. the opposite of staples or necessities: *l*_____

5. item of trade or use: *c*_____

6. a beverage made by cooking something in water: *b*_____

7. the people who plan revolutions: *r*_____

THE DECAFÉ

Drawing by Stevens; © 1986 The New Yorker Magazine, Inc.

IT WORKS!
Learning Strategy:
Expressing Your
Opinion

TASK 7: THE COFFEE FORUM

What do you think about drinking coffee? Is it a pleasant social ritual? A quick aid to waking up in the morning? An enjoyable and soothing break from work or study? Or is it a harmful addiction? A waste of time and money? Is it a junk-food drink? Do you like decaffeinated (without caffeine) coffee? Think about this popular brew. Write a statement of your view of coffee. Be prepared to read your statement and defend your opinion.

TASK 8: FOOD FANTASY

Write a paragraph about your dream or ideal of the perfect meal. Compare with the class or in a group.

LOOKING BACK ON CHAPTER 4

Stop for a moment to look back at the goals for this chapter. How many have you accomplished? How much are you doing to improve your language skills? What have you learned about different cultures? Complete the following crossword puzzle to review some key vocabulary from this chapter.

VOCABULARY REVIEW: CROSSWORD PUZZLE

Do the crossword puzzle on page 89 to review key vocabulary from Chapter 4. Fill in the squares with the letters of words that fit the descriptions. Put only one letter in each square. The first letter of each word is given. After you finish, take the letters of the squares with the heavy lines, put them in the right order in the blanks, and find out the *mystery word*. (Answers are in the Answer Appendix at the end of the book, but don't look them up until you've given it a good try!)
Mystery Word: The most expressive way in the English language to say that food tastes good: __ __ __!

ACROSS (left to right)

3. forbidden
4. meat from a pig
5. one who doesn't eat meat
7. timetable, word pronounced differently in Canada and U.S.
9. combination of breakfast and lunch
10. from a particular cultural tradition, as an ___ restaurant
11. variety, quality of being made up of different parts
14. Some say that good and bad taste are ___.
15. a green leafy vegetable used in salads
16. pieces of paper that give you money or a reduction in price of a product
19. what you should keep off the table
20. little round green or purple fruits

DOWN

1. troubling, disturbing as in an ____ moment
2. foods you use every day
6. past of the verb *eat*
8. implements used for eating, as knives, forks, spoons, etc.
11. a treat, a special food
12. a ceremony, set of actions
13. a common Mexican dish
17. beginning, start; where something comes from
18. one of the key words for courtesy in English

How, When, and Why Do We Celebrate?

Every culture celebrates some special days. The flow of time seems to stop while work and the normal routine are put aside. People make special food, decorate their homes, and participate in rituals or ceremonies in honor of some person or idea. What do you want to know about holidays in North America? Why and how are they celebrated? Where did they come from? How do they compare with important holidays in your country? First, take a look. This chapter begins with calendars and the dates of major holidays in the United States and Canada. Then it looks more closely at some of them. Perhaps when you understand more about North American holidays, you will join in the celebrations.

Now think about some goals for your own improvement.

To learn more about:

• Types of calendars used around the world
• Important holidays in the U.S.A. and Canada
• Similarities and differences among holidays in various cultures
• How new holidays come to be
• The effects of prejudice and discrimination
• Giving gifts and cards in North America

To practice skills:

• Categorizing material (putting it in categories)
• Showing comparisons and contrasts on charts
• Writing about beliefs and feelings in a journal
• Making predictions about the contents of a reading
• Finding common reasons for diverse customs

To acquire new vocabulary

THEME 1: HOLIDAYS AROUND THE WORLD

What makes holidays so special? Holidays seem full of magic because they replace work and our normal routine with color and music. The food, clothing, decorations, and rituals vary greatly from one culture to another. But if we look more closely, can we find similarities underneath these differences?

A. Three Different Calendars

Calendars are used to control and measure time. Americans and Canadians use the European calendar, but different calendars are used in some other cultures. Look at the illustrations of three of them. Read the descriptions of these calendars and try to find similarities and differences.

The European Calendar. The European calendar is used in many parts of the world. It was finished in 1582. It is a solar calendar because it is based on the movement of the earth around the sun. The European calendar has seven days per week and twelve months per year. All months have thirty or thirty-one days, except for February which usually has twenty-eight. Three years in a row have 365 days, and every fourth year has an extra day, February 29th. The fourth year is called a "leap year." Because of this adjustment, the months stay in the same season, year after year.

The Muslim Calendar. The Muslim calendar is used in many parts of the Islamic World. It is over 1,300 years old. It is a lunar calendar because it is based on the movement of the moon around the earth. The Muslim calendar has twelve months per year, with the months alternating between thirty days and twenty-nine days long. Most years have 354 days, but some have 355 days. The months do not stay in the same season each year. The ninth month of the Muslim calendar is Ramadan, a special month of fasting and prayer.

The Chinese Calendar. The Chinese calendar is one of the oldest in the world, and dates back over 2,000 or 3,000 years. It is used in China, Japan, Korea, Vietnam, and other countries. The year is divided into twelve lunar months, alternating between "big months" of thirty days and "small months" of twenty-nine days. Every few years, some extra months are added to keep up with the solar year. For this reason, the Chinese calendar can be called both a lunar and a solar calendar. The months stay in the same season every year.

Threads

Over 970 million people worldwide believe in Islam.

TASK 1: COMPARING AND CONTRASTING CALENDARS

Fill in the chart. Compare your answers with those of your classmates.

CHART OF SIMILARITIES AND DIFFERENCES AMONG CALENDARS

	EUROPEAN	MUSLIM	CHINESE
1. Number of months per year	_____	_____	_____
2. Number of days per month	_____	_____	_____
3. Solar or lunar?	_____	_____	_____
4. How old?	_____	_____	_____
5. Months stay with the same seasons or change?	_____	_____	_____

TASK 2: TALKING IT OVER

1. Which calendar is used in your culture? Is more than one used?
2. What divisions are there? Days, weeks, months, years, others? Do the divisions have names or numbers? How do they relate to the European calendar?
3. What are the four seasons of the year in Europe and North America? Which one has two names? How are the seasons in your culture similar to those in North America? How are they different?
4. In North America there is a day on the calendar that is considered unlucky. That day is Friday the 13th. It doesn't matter what month it occurs. In Spain and Latin America, the tradition is a little different. The day of bad luck is Tuesday (not Friday) the 13th. Are there any unlucky days in your culture? Are there any lucky days?
5. What is leap year? Why is it necessary in the European calendar? In North America there is an old custom about leap year. February 29th has been the day when it is customary for a woman to invite a man out on a date, or even to propose marriage! What do you think of this custom? Is there any custom like it in your culture?

TASK 3: GUESSING THE ORIGINS FOR THE NAMES OF THE DAYS

Where do the names for the days come from in your culture? The English ones come from the gods honored in olden times. Read the following descriptions. Then think of the days of the week: Sunday, Monday, Tuesday, and so on. Guess which sentence gives the origin for each one.

1. *Freya* is the name of the ancient Norse goddess of love.
2. The sun was honored by people in Europe long ago.
3. *Thor* is the name of the ancient Norse god of thunder.
4. The old Roman god of agriculture was called *Saturn*.
5. The moon was honored by people in Europe long ago.
6. To the ancient Norse people, *Woden* was the king of the gods.
7. *Tiw* was the old Anglo Saxon name for the Greek god of war.

B. The Yearly Cycle of Holidays

The holiday wheel in the illustration shows major holidays in Canada and the United States. Both countries use the European calendar and share many of the same traditions. As you can see, some holidays are exactly the same in both countries, some are similar, and some are completely different.

In general, holidays all over the world fall into six categories. These categories are traditional (passed down from long ago), patriotic (honoring an important moment in a nation's history), religious, seasonal, showing love and appreciation, and honoring heroes.

U.S. and Canadian Holidays*

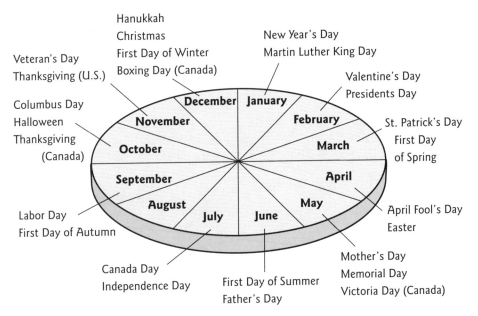

*(Not all holidays included)

Managing Your Learning: Categorizing material makes it easier to understand and study.

TASK 1: CATEGORIZING HOLIDAYS

Categorizing means separating things and putting them into groups or categories. It is a useful skill for organizing material. Study the holiday wheel. Use the name of each holiday to guess its category. Some might be in more than one. List the holidays in the chart below. Put a check in the right square to show if they are celebrated in the U.S., Canada, or both. Compare answers with your classmates.

NORTH AMERICAN HOLIDAY CHART

	NAME OF HOLIDAY	U.S.	CANADA	BOTH
traditional	_____	_____	_____	_____
patriotic	_____	_____	_____	_____
religious	_____	_____	_____	_____
seasonal	_____	_____	_____	_____
showing love and appreciation	_____	_____	_____	_____
honoring heroes	_____	_____	_____	_____

TASK 2: COMPARING AND CONTRASTING HOLIDAYS ACROSS CULTURES

Work in pairs or groups of three. Complete a holiday wheel like the one below with major holidays from your own culture(s). Then talk about the following questions. Share your answers with the class.

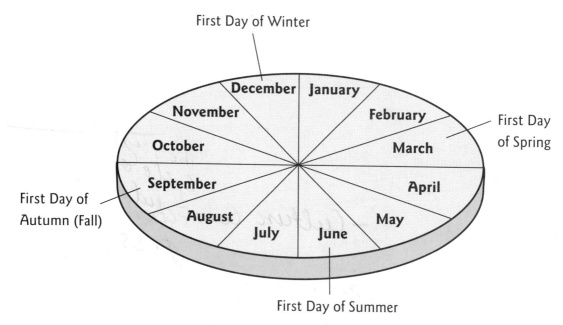

1. What kinds of holidays are most common in your culture(s) (seasonal, patriotic, etc.)?
2. Are there other reasons for holidays? In your culture, do you celebrate when a person reaches a certain age? Is there a holiday in honor of the dead, or for people from certain professions?
3. What months or seasons have the most holidays?
4. Compare your wheel with the U.S./Canada wheel. What similarities and differences do you find?

YOUR PERSONAL JOURNAL:
DESCRIBING A HOLIDAY FROM THE PAST

Take a trip in your imagination backwards in time. Think about a holiday celebration when you were a child. Try to see it "in your mind's eye." Many North American children believe in Santa Claus and the Easter Bunny, magical figures who bring them gifts if they are good. Did you believe in any magical figures or happenings? What emotions did you feel? How have your beliefs and feelings changed? How old were you at the time? How old were your parents, relatives, and friends? Write about the holiday, your beliefs and your emotions. Later you may use part of this description for another assignment or to read to the class.

THEME 2: CELEBRATING THE BEGINNING OF A NEW YEAR

No matter what calendar is used, the start of a New Year is a magical time. It is a moment of transition, change, and opportunity. All things seem possible. In the United States and Canada, decorations generally include the New Year pictured as a baby and the Old Year as an old man, often called "Father Time."

On December 31, the last day of the year, called *New Year's Eve,* many North Americans give parties for their friends. These parties are usually for separate age groups. The adults go to their party, teenagers to

A crowd gets ready to make noise at midnight to celebrate the new year in Times Square.

theirs, and small children often stay home with babysitters. Some adults go to nightclubs to watch a show and greet the new year. It is customary to have a countdown during the last minute or two before midnight. Then everyone makes noise. Sometimes people form a circle and sing the traditional old Scottish song, *Auld Lang Syne* (see page 100), which means "Good Old Times."

TASK 1: PICTURE THE DIFFERENCE

Look at the photo on page 99. What are people doing to celebrate the New Year? Imagine people in your culture on New Year's Eve. Draw a picture to show their celebration. (If you cannot draw very well, use stick figures and labels, or write a *word picture*.) Explain your picture to a small group or to the class.

TASK 2: COMPARING AND CONTRASTING NEW YEAR'S CELEBRATIONS

The following list shows the New Year activities of many (though not all) Canadians and Americans. Make an X in the correct column to show what people in your culture do or don't do to celebrate New Year. Then write a comment to explain the differences or similarities. Share the list and comments with your classmates.

*IT WORKS!
Learning Strategy:
Looking for
Similarities and
Differences*

COMPARING NEW YEAR CELEBRATIONS

ACTIVITIES	SAME	DIFFERENT	COMMENTS
1. Spend the evening with friends (rather than family)			
2. Go to a big party			
3. Drink alcohol (often a lot)			
4. Dance			
5. Watch television while waiting for midnight			
6. Wear funny hats			

ACTIVITIES	SAME	DIFFERENT	COMMENTS
7. Blow whistles and noisemakers			
8. Kiss at 12 midnight			
9. Make resolutions (promises for good behavior during the coming year)			
10. Suffer from a hangover* on January 1st			

*The sick feeling, often with headache and vomiting, that people get after drinking too much alcohol.

TASK 3: CONSIDERING DIFFERENT POINTS OF VIEW ABOUT ALCOHOL

Many North Americans enjoy drinking wine, beer, or liquor (such as whiskey, brandy, gin, rum, or vodka) during holiday celebrations. They feel that drinking alcohol makes them more relaxed. In recent years, however, the general attitude toward alcohol has changed in the United States and Canada. There used to be more heavy drinkers. Nowadays, there are more moderate drinkers. What happens during celebrations in your culture? Are alcoholic drinks or another kind of drug served? Do men and women drink alcohol? Older people and younger people? Have attitudes changed? Think about your family and friends from your culture. Write down an opinion about alcohol from *their* point of view. Then write down your own personal opinion. Share and compare opinions in small groups or with the class.

Opinion of my family or friends:

_____

_____

My own personal opinion:

_____

_____

TASK 4: MUSIC FOR THE NEW YEAR

Look at the words and music to the traditional New Year song, *Auld Lang Syne*. It was written over a hundred years ago by the famous poet of Scotland, Robert Burns. Can you understand the basic meaning? Try to learn how to sing it. If you can, bring in some music from your own culture's New Year's celebration to share with the class.

Auld Lang Syne

Should auld acquaintance be forgot,
   and never brought to mind?
Should auld acquaintance be forgot
   and days of Auld Lang Syne.
For Auld Lang Syne, my dear,
   for Auld Lang Syne
We'll take a cup of kindness yet
   for Auld Lang Syne.

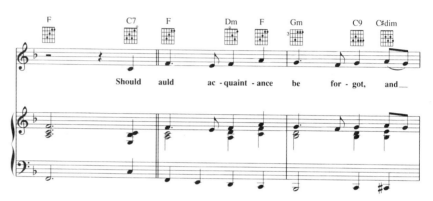

TASK 5: MAKING NEW YEAR'S RESOLUTIONS

Making New Year's resolutions is an old custom in the United States and Canada. These resolutions are promises to ourselves about goals for improvement. They usually involve the breaking of bad habits (eating junk food, losing our temper, postponing work). We try to change to good habits (eating good food, controlling our temper, finishing work on time).

Imagine it is New Year's Day. Make up five resolutions, using the words *will* and *won't*. For example: *I will stop smoking. I won't be late for class.*

Afterwards, compare with your classmates. What is the most common resolution? Which is the most unusual? Do you think everyone will keep these resolutions?

THEME 3: HOW A NEW HOLIDAY COMES TO BE

Most holidays are celebrated because of old traditions. But sometimes a new holiday is created. Can you think of a new holiday from your culture? What was the reason for it?

On October 27, 1982, Canada changed the name of its national patriotic holiday on July 1st from *Dominion Day* to *Canada Day*. Six months earlier, the Constitution (the official document of Canadian law) had been brought to Canada from England. This symbolized another step in the gradual change of Canada from British colony, to Self Rule (in 1867), to independent nation. The new name of the holiday was a symbol to show that Canada is truly independent.

The most recent change in U.S. holidays was the creation of a completely new one to honor the civil rights leader, Dr. Martin Luther King. To learn more about this, read the following selection from the book, *About Martin Luther King Day.*

GET READY TO READ: USING THE TITLE AND PHOTO TO PREDICT A READING

Look at the title and the photo. Read the caption underneath the photo. Then use what you have learned to choose the correct way to complete this statement about the reading.

The reading will show that it was (easy, somewhat hard, very hard) to get people to accept a holiday in honor of Dr. Martin Luther King.

After you finish reading, see if your prediction about the selection was correct.

GET READY TO READ: SCANNING FOR VOCABULARY

The following selection contains various words related to government and to civil rights. Complete the following exercise to learn some of these words in advance. Don't expect to understand everything.

1. American and Canadian government has three levels: national, state or provincial, and local. In the first paragraph, find a word beginning with *f* that describes something related to the national government: _____.

2. In the second paragraph, find a short word that means a proposal for a law: _____.

3. The meeting of the people who make the laws is called the *Congress.* The U.S. Congress consists of two different groups, commonly called the House and the Senate. Find the full name of the House, given in the second paragraph. It is called: the House _____ _____.

4. Another name for the Congress is the *Legislature.* This word means any group of lawmakers and can also refer to the parliament in Canada and other countries. Find two related words, similar to *legislature,* with the following meanings: (1) the men and women who make the laws, _____, and (2) the act of making a law or the law itself, _____.

5. In the second half of the reading, scan for two words that relate to civil rights. Find the word beginning with *p* that means *a negative feeling or judgment someone has against people just because they are from another race or group:* _____. Then find the word beginning with *d* that means *bad treatment of people just because they are from another race or group:* _____. Do you think these two always go together? Explain.

Making it a holiday

by Mary Virginia Fox

On the third Monday in January,* schools are closed. Postal workers and bankers get the day off. Every federal office in the country shuts down. It is a day for parades, speeches, and prayers. On this day we honor Martin Luther King, Jr. We remember the changes that he brought about in this country and around the world. It took an act of Congress to make this day a national holiday. More than 15 years went by from the death of Martin Luther King Jr. before legislation was passed.

First, a bill had to be introduced by a member of the House of Representatives. The Speaker of the House then assigned the bill to a committee, and the members of the committee discussed the matter in detail. Meetings were held where people with opposing ideas could state their positions. The committee finally reported that they felt the bill should be put to a vote. Still another group of legislators, the Rules committee, had to schedule the debate on the issue.

When the House of Representatives passed the bill by a vote of 338 to 90, it was sent to the Senate. Here again, the issue had to pass through committee discussion and public hearings before a final vote was taken.

The final difficulty to honoring King was overcome on October 4, 1983. Senator Jesse Helms, from the state of North Carolina, gave up his one-man fight to defeat the bill.

Why was anyone against having the holiday? Some people pointed out that only two other individuals, George Washington and Christopher Columbus, were honored by national holidays. Why hadn't Abraham Lincoln,† Franklin Delano Roosevelt, Dwight Eisenhower, or John F. Kennedy, all great Americans, been given such an honor?

Other critics said if we were trying to make up for the bad treatment of blacks during slavery, we should also honor an Indian hero too. These people had also suffered prejudice. King's admirers pointed out that he was great because he tried to bring about social change through peaceful means, not by war or revolution.

Those who still opposed the idea claimed that we had enough holidays. This would make the tenth. The Congressional Budget office estimated it would cost $18 million for extra overtime pay to federal employees who had to work on a federal holiday. Another $220 million would be needed to pay employees for a day on which they were not working.

Senator Robert Dole said, "I suggest they hurry back to their pocket calculators and estimate the cost of 300 years of slavery, followed by a century or more of economic, political, and social . . . discrimination."

---

*In the U.S., some national holidays occur on a fixed date, like Independence Day which is always July 4th. Others are celebrated on the Monday nearest the original date of the holiday. These are called *observed holidays*. They are made for the convenience of working people, giving them three-day weekends.

†The third Monday in February used to honor George Washington, the first President of the U.S., but this was changed recently. Now it is called President's Day, and it honors both George Washington and Abraham Lincoln.

Martin Luther King Jr. (1929–1968) was a Christian clergyman and a leader in the U.S. civil rights movement. This was a movement for the equality of all people, without distinction of race, sex, or religion. Dr. King was strongly influenced by the ideas of the great Indian thinker, Mahatma Ghandi. In 1964, Martin Luther King won the Nobel Peace Prize for his leadership of the nonviolent struggle for racial equality. He was shot to death by an assassin's bullet in Memphis, Tennessee, on April 4, 1968.

In every session of Congress following Dr. King's assassination, members had introduced legislation calling for the holiday. Even before the holiday was official, many blacks took it upon themselves to stay home from school or work on January 15. Thousands wrote letters and signed petitions of support. On January 15, 1981, one hundred thousand marchers met in Washington, D.C. to show their support for the holiday.

The bill was finally passed by both the House of Representatives and the Senate and was signed into law by President Reagan on November 2, 1983.

TASK 1: CHECKING COMPREHENSION

Tell if each statement is true or false, according to the reading selection. Write *T* or *F* in the space provided. Then explain your choice.

1. _____ Martin Luther King Day is now an official holiday in the U.S.
2. _____ It was easy to pass a holiday through the U.S. legislature to honor Dr. King.
3. _____ Senator Jesse Helms from North Carolina was one of Martin Luther King's great supporters.
4. _____ Some people against the Martin Luther King holiday wanted a holiday named for John F. Kennedy.
5. _____ When a holiday was named for Martin Luther King, another holiday was also named for an Indian hero.
6. _____ Senator Robert Dole thought that the Martin Luther King holiday would cost too much.
7. _____ Probably some of the people against this holiday were against it because of a prejudice against blacks.
8. _____ Many people celebrated the Martin Luther King holiday even before it became an official holiday.

> **Threads**
>
> 18% of employers grant paid leave on Martin Luther King, Jr., Day, 16% for Columbus Day, and 45% for Presidents' Day.

TASK 2: TALKING IT OVER

1. Why did the United States create a new holiday called Martin Luther King Day?
2. What other groups are there, besides black Americans, who suffer from discrimination? What groups in your culture have this problem?
3. Have you ever suffered from discrimination? If so, where and when?
4. "Everybody has some prejudices." True or false? Explain.
5. Can you think of another hero who has helped a minority group in some culture?
6. What is a hero? Can a woman be a hero? Why or why not?

TASK 3: WHAT ARE THE ROOTS OF PREJUDICE?

Finish the following statement. Compare with your classmates.

In my opinion, prejudice and discrimination exist because . . .

_____

_____

_____

In your journal, write about a hero you admire. (To *admire* means to look up to, to think highly of.) Choose a national or regional hero from your culture, or a personal hero. As you write, try to answer these questions:

1. Who was or is this person?
2. What role did he or she play in your country or region or group? Was it political, religious, economic, or in the social structure?
3. What exactly did this person do?
4. Why do people think this person is a hero?
5. Why do *you* think he or she is important?

TASK 4: OUTSIDE ASSIGNMENTS

A. Louis Riel was an important figure in Canadian history who also fought for the rights of a minority group. Go to the library and find some information about him. Or work on another Canadian or American hero. Prepare a description of this person to share with the class.
B. Martin Luther King, Jr. was one of the most famous orators (speechmakers) of the twentieth century. Try to find a tape of one of his speeches, such as "I Have a Dream" or "I Have Gone to the Mountain." Bring it to class and listen to part of it with your classmates.

TASK 5: RELATING THE READING TO OTHER KNOWLEDGE

In the reading *Making It a Law,* there are several references to different parts of the U.S. government. Would you like to know more about government in the United States? Look at the chart below and read the caption. Can you understand how a bill becomes a law? Is this process similar to the one in your culture's government?

This chart shows the three branches of the U.S. government and the highest officials in each branch. All three branches of government are involved in making laws. Here is a very simple explanation of the process: The legislative branch votes on bills (possible new laws). The president signs bills into law. The judicial branch decides if laws are constitutional (correct according to the U.S. Constitution).

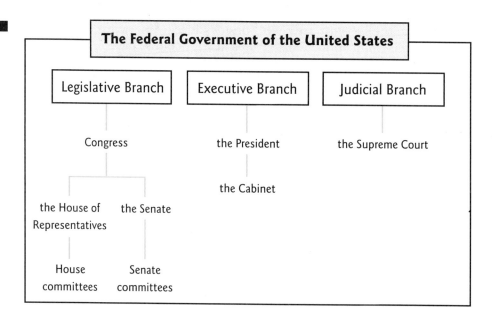

The Federal Government of the United States

Legislative Branch	Executive Branch	Judicial Branch
Congress	the President	the Supreme Court
	the Cabinet	

the House of Representatives   the Senate

House committees   Senate committees

Holidays transform ordinary life with the magic of fine foods, fancy clothing, rituals, symbols, cards and presents, singing and dancing, and colorful decorations. Underneath all of this, each celebration has its own unique and special meaning. Let's take a look at both the outside (customs, decorations and such) and the inside (emotion, meaning) of some holidays.

A. Creating Holiday Magic

Throughout the year there are special times for showing love and appreciation. Valentine's Day, February 14th, is the most romantic one in North America. On this day, people show their love for one another with gifts of cards, flowers, or candies. It is also a big day to become engaged or to be married. Look at the greeting cards in the illustration. Which one is a valentine? What holidays are the others for? Who do you think is sending them? To whom?

TASK 1: TALKING IT OVER

1. When do people in your culture send greeting cards?
2. Can you guess which North American holidays (major and minor) have the following special colors?
   a. red and white   c. red and green
   b. green   d. orange and black
3. What holidays in your culture have special colors?
4. Can you guess which North American holidays have the following symbols:
   a. a rabbit   c. a pumpkin with a face
   b. a fir or pine tree with lights   d. a heart
5. What symbols are important for holidays in your culture? Why?
6. In North America, people usually open a gift right away when they receive it. Is that also customary in your culture?

TASK 2: WHAT PRESENT SHOULD I GIVE?

Gift giving is different across cultures. In North America, when should you give a present? What should you give? As a class or in groups, talk about the following situations. Decide if a gift is necessary. If so, what should it be? Here are some possibilities.

A bottle of wine	jewelry
a souvenir from your country	flowers
an expensive shirt or blouse	candy
a special food you've made	a book

a. Your school or business office has arranged for you to spend Thanksgiving Day with a family. You don't know these people.
b. You are invited to a Halloween party organized by the International Club
c. You are going to visit a friend in the hospital.
d. You are invited to a Fourth of July or Canada Day barbecue at the home of your teacher

TASK 3: THE WORD-TO-SENTENCE GAME

Just for fun, practice building sentences from random (unplanned) words. They won't be perfect. They don't have to make much sense. A volunteer goes to the board to write the words. Another person begins by naming a holiday and pointing to someone. That person says the first word that "pops into his or her mind," then points to someone else. After six words, everyone stops and tries to write a sentence with all the words. The one with the best sentence wins, and begins again by naming a holiday . . .

MODEL: Valentine's Day—heart—candy—red—gift—work—mess

On Valentine's day a boy at work gave me a gift of a red heart filled with candy, but it fell and made a mess.

TASK 4: OUTSIDE ASSIGNMENT: LOOKING AT CARDS

Look at the card section in a drugstore or other store. How many different kinds of holiday cards are there right now? Which ones are funny? Copy down the words of some of your favorites and share them with your classmates.

TASK 5: WRITE A POEM!

Here's a traditional little Valentine poem that is very well known:

> Roses are red,
> Violets are blue.
> Sugar is sweet,
> And so are you.

Students in North America sometimes make fun of this traditional poem. The "game" is to change the third (and sometimes the fourth) line. The rhyme must stay the same. This is one common variation:

> Roses are red,
> Violets are blue.
> You look like a monkey,
> And you smell like one too!

Just for fun, make up your own version of the poem. It can be serious, or silly, whatever you wish.

YOUR PERSONAL JOURNAL: WRITING ABOUT HOMESICKNESS

*IT WORKS!
Learning Strategy:
Expressing Your
Options*

Holidays are often difficult times for international students. It's hard to be away from your family and friends during a special time. Holidays can bring on a lot of homesickness.

Almost anyone who lives far away from family and close friends gets homesick. Some people cover it up better than others. Homesickness is a normal reaction to being separated from your loved ones. It becomes a problem if it begins to cause trouble with your school or work.

One way to cope (keep on going) with homesickness is to share your feelings with other people. Often you'll find that others feel the same way you do.

Use your journal to describe some experiences you or a friend have had with homesickness. Try to write for at least 20 to 30 minutes about the feelings you've experienced. Some may be related to holidays, and others to different occasions.

Later, share one of your stories with your teacher, the class, or a small group.

B. Looking for the Deeper Meaning of Holidays

One way to understand our own culture better is by studying other cultures. This sounds odd, but it is true. Comparing holidays from two cultures can give us an insight (flash of understanding) into their real meaning by showing us how they meet the same human needs in different ways.

Read the following selection, comparing a North American holiday with a Mexican one.

GET READY TO READ: VOCABULARY PREVIEW

Learn the following words—most of them *spooky* (referring to spirits and scary things)—before reading the selection.

cemetery	graveyard; place for burying the dead.
coffin	box for a dead body
costume	clothing to make someone look very different, perhaps like a certain animal or type of person
ghost	spirit of a dead person who comes back to earth
skeleton	the bones of a human body
skull	bony framework of the head

Comparing Halloween and the Day of the Dead

by John C. Condon

Compare two holidays which share a common religious past and come at the same time on the calendar—Halloween in the United States and the Day of the Dead in Mexico. In the United States there are ghosts and skeletons that appear that day, but they are mostly symbolic, like the colors orange and black which show it is Halloween. Or they appear in costumes worn by children. These children go door to door looking for what the day really means to them, a chance to get treasures of candy.

In Mexico, the Day of the Dead (*Día de los Muertos*) is a time to commune with the dead. Special breads are prepared; candy skulls and coffins

are made. Some of these are personalized with the names of the people who are going to eat them. Songs are sung, humorous poems are given out in the streets which tell about death dancing with the rich and the powerful, the Pope, the President, as well as the ordinary person. Meals are set for the dead at many homes, and the cemeteries take on a festive air.

Good Neighbors

TASK 1: CHECKING COMPREHENSION

Complete the following statements according to the reading.

1. On Halloween in the U.S., ghosts and skeletons appear as symbols and also in _____.

2. The children there go _____.

3. The real meaning of the holiday for them is _____.

4. In Mexico, the Day of the Dead is a time to _____.

5. Candies are made in the shapes of _____.

6. Songs and poems tell about _____.

7. In many homes, meals are set for _____.

TASK 2: TALKING IT OVER

1. Do you like to dress up in a costume? Are there holidays in your culture when you can do this?

2. Would you like to eat a candy skull or coffin with your name on it? Why do you think the Mexicans do this?

3. How are the two holidays similar?

4. How are they different?

5. Are either of these similar in any way to a holiday from your culture? Explain.

6. Do you like to get scared sometimes? Do you ever go to *thrillers* (scary movies)? Why do you think these are so popular?

TASK 3: IDIOMS TO USE WITH HOLIDAYS

Look at the examples on the next page. They show humorous illustrations of three idioms and suggest their real meanings. Think about the holidays described in this chapter. Then decide in what holiday situations you could say the idioms, and use them in good sentences.

Guessing the Meaning of Three New Idioms

1. She fell in love.

2. My eyes were
   bigger than
   my stomach.

3. He's pulling your leg!

TASK 4: HOLIDAY PHOTOS

The following photos show North Americans celebrating holidays. Think back to an important holiday in your childhood. Perhaps you wrote about it already in your journal. Compare it with one of the holidays in the photos. Tell how it is similar and how it is different. Then tell what you think the meaning or importance of the holiday is. Fill in the comparison chart that follows the descriptions and photos.

Thanksgiving

In the United States and Canada, the harvest festival is called Thanksgiving. It is a family day. People often travel long distances to go home on this day. The traditional meal includes turkey and cranberry sauce, two foods given to the early settlers by the Indians long ago. In the U.S., a group called the Pilgrims came in 1620 to escape religious discrimination. They found the first winter very hard and many died. In the spring the Indians taught them to hunt and plant corn. In the fall they celebrated the harvest. The tradition in Canada is even older. A group of settlers, led by Sir Martin Frobisher, arrived in Newfoundland in 1578. After a long and dangerous sea journey, they celebrated their safe arrival in the new country with a thanksgiving feast.

Christmas

On December 25th of each year, Christians the world over celebrate the birth of Jesus Christ. They decorate Christmas trees, sing Christmas carols (songs) and set up cribs (a stable with a poor bed of straw and figures of Jesus and others) to show the Christmas story. According to

Threads

In 1990, Americans purchased 2.3 billion Christmas cards and mailed about 44 cards per family.

tradition, Jesus Christ was the son of God. But he chose to be born in a poor stable for animals. Three Wise Men from the East came to see him and brought him gifts. They followed a magic star that appeared in the sky to show them the way. Some poor shepherds also saw the star and came. Perhaps that is why people give presents on Christmas day.

Victoria Day

May 24th is Victoria Day in Canada, a celebration of the birthday of Queen Victoria of England who ruled for over 50 years and died in 1900. Canada is unique in the Americas because it gained its independence without violence. Canadians are proud of their independence (and celebrate it on July 1st with fireworks and picnics), but most of them do not mind that there are still some ties to the British Queen. Many like to continue old customs and still give honor to the Queen of England. Traditionally, in the Western provinces, this is the day for planting flowers.

Independence Day

July 4th in the United States honors the signing of the Declaration of Independence from England in 1776. A war followed, called the American Revolution, and many people had to fight and die to gain the right to begin a new country. The customary way of celebrating is with parades, eating, drinking, and fireworks

COMPARISON CHART OF HOLIDAYS

1. I am comparing the holiday from my culture: _____

2. With the North American holiday: _____

3. Similarities:

_____

_____

_____

_____

4. Differences:

_____

_____

_____

_____

5. In my opinion, the meaning of these holidays is:

_____

_____

_____

_____

IT WORKS!
Learning Strategy:
Looking for
Similarities and
Differences

LOOKING BACK ON CHAPTER 5

Think about what you have learned in this chapter about North American holidays. Look at the goals at the beginning. Which ones were really important? Are you speaking, reading, and writing English better than before? Can you understand more when English is spoken? Do the exercises that follow to review some key vocabulary from this chapter. (Answers are given in the Answer Appendix at the end of the book.)

VOCABULARY REVIEW: SCRAMBLED LETTERS

Unscramble the letters to make some of the key words and phrases from Chapter 5. A hint (short suggestion) is given by each one to help you guess it.

1. WEN RAYE TORNIULSEOS
2. GARVNHOE
3. NALRU DAALCREN
4. JEEPDURIC

5. APEL ERAY

6. LITSNAVEEN YAD
7. TOTRIPACI
8. OT LUPL ROYU GEL

What people make and break.
The result of too much alcohol.
One way of measuring the year.
A negative judgment with no
    basis in fact.
What makes the months stay in
    place.
Very romantic!
Honoring your country.
To fool you.

VOCABULARY REVIEW: WORD FAMILIES

Fill in the missing members of the word families. The first one is done for you.

VERB	-ING FORM	NOUN
1. participate	participating	participation
2. _____	_____	category
3. predict	_____	_____
4. _____	_____	legislature
5. celebrate	_____	_____
6. _____	creating	_____
7. _____	_____	decoration
8. _____	discriminating	_____
9. appreciate	_____	_____

VOCABULARY REVIEW: TRANSFORMATIONS

Change the nouns to adjectives. The first one is done for you.

1. tradition _traditional_
2. person _____
3. season _____
4. symbol _____
5. independence _____

6. magic _____
7. use _____
8. custom _____
9. luck _____
10. nation _____

What Are the Secrets of Good Health?

INTRODUCTION

Every culture has its own view of health and medicine. The conventional (ordinary, common) medicine of the West is practiced in many parts of the world, with certain cultural differences. This tradition includes the use of surgery (operations) and drugs, in the form of pills and injections. But in North America and Europe today, some forms of alternative (different, unusual) medicine are gaining in popularity. Americans and Canadians are changing their attitudes toward illness in other ways too. There is a growing awareness of the important roles of lifestyle and the emotions in the process of healing.

Think about some goals for your own improvement.

To learn more about:

• Some kinds of mainstream and alternative medicine
• Different cultural views of what it means to be healthy
• Ways of coping with sickness
• Changing attitudes in North America about illness and lifestyle
• The relationship between our emotions and our health

To practice skills:

• Working with a partner to solve problems
• Giving an oral summary of conclusions
• Expressing opinions in a group
• Guessing the meanings of vocabulary from context
• Identifying and describing emotions
• Making a graph of emotional ups and downs

To acquire new vocabulary

THEME 1: MAINSTREAM AND ALTERNATIVE MEDICINE

Health is a big business in the United States and Canada. Every city and town has hospitals, clinics, and doctors' offices. They are part of the system of *conventional* or *mainstream* medicine. (*Mainstream* means "representing the usual practice of most people.") However, even good doctors sometimes make mistakes. Operations and drugs have *side effects* (other changes produced in the patient besides helping the illness). So a number of North Americans choose other forms of medicine. Some of them use plants and animal products to cure people. Some use exercise or massage or rituals. In North America, these different medical practices are generally called *alternative medicine*.

116

A. Some Different Forms of Healing

Conventional medicine is by far the most important type of health care in North America today. But many forms of alternative medicine are gaining acceptance. Look at the photos and read their captions. Then answer the questions that follow.

TASK 1: TALKING IT OVER

1. Which of these types of medicine is most familiar to you? What kinds of medicine are practiced in your culture?
2. Do you know of anyone who has been helped (or hurt) by one of them? Which of the four would you prefer?
3. Many North Americans go to their family doctor for a checkup every year, whether they feel sick or not. Do people in your culture do this too? What do you think of the annual checkup?
4. Which of these kinds of alternative medicine have you heard of: chiropractors, meditation, yoga, tai chi, homeopathy?
5. In your opinion, why do many North Americans choose alternative medicine? Would you choose it?

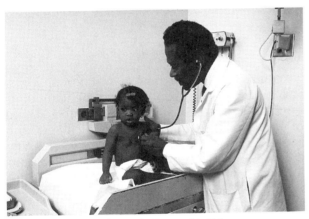

Conventional Western Medicine

Natural Healing with Herbs and Animal Products

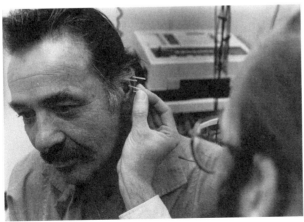

Acupuncture

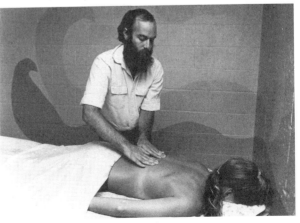

Massage Therapy

Managing Your Learning: Working with a partner to solve problems is a good way to practice two-way conversation in English.

TASK 2: WHAT DO YOU RECOMMEND FOR CHRONIC PROBLEMS?

Work with a partner. Take turns reading from the list of chronic problems (problems that go on for a long time). Decide on a recommendation for each one. Should the sick person go to the hospital or the doctor? Should he or she try some form of massage or other alternative medicine? Or can you think of another remedy? (A *remedy* is something that cures us.) Be prepared to make a comment to the class afterwards about the decisions you make together.

a. A person with a constant backache or pain in the neck
b. Someone very skinny with no appetite
c. Someone suffering from depression (a continual feeling of deep sadness for no special reason)
d. A person who gets headaches every day
e. A person with no energy who feels tired all the time
f. Someone who walks in his/her sleep
g. Someone who feels sick to his/her stomach after eating

TASK 3: GUESSING THE MEANING OF IDIOMS

Look at the idiomatic expressions and guess their meanings.

Threads

A good laugh and a long sleep are the best cures in the doctor's book.

Irish proverb

Idiomatic Expressions for Telling How You Feel

Here are some common ways of answering the questions: *How are you?* or *How are you feeling?*

I'm feeling . . .

1. Down. (in bad spirits)
Run-down. (tired
and weak)

2. Under the weather.

3. On top of the world.

4. Like a million dollars. (Imagine your own drawing.)

Which idioms would you use when you are feeling good? When you are feeling bad? Think about some idiomatic ways of saying you feel good or bad in your culture and try to explain them in English.

TASK 4: COMPLETING DESCRIPTIONS

Work with the class. Sit in a circle. One person starts by using one of the idioms to say how he or she feels, and gives a reason. The next person uses the same idiom but gives another reason, and so on until five or six reasons have been given. Then, change to a new idiom and continue. Use your imagination to think up many reasons.

EXAMPLE: I'm feeling on top of the world because

. . . I just got a letter from home.

. . . I bought a new jacket.

. . . a friend invited me to dinner.

B. Cultural Differences in Conventional Medicine

Everyone knows about the wonderful triumphs of modern conventional medicine. The terrible disease of smallpox has been eliminated through vaccination. Aspirins, antibiotics, and certain operations are accepted and used all over the world. Conventional medicine is based on science. But does the word *science* mean the same thing everywhere?

The following selection is from the book *Medicine and Culture* by Lynn Payer, an American who lived in Europe for many years. It tells of the big differences in conventional medicine in four countries: England, the United States, France, and Germany.

GET READY TO READ: LEARNING USEFUL MEDICAL VOCABULARY

Study the list of common medical terms that appear in the reading selection. Then use them to complete the paragraph. This will help you to understand the reading.

MEDICAL TERMS	DEFINITIONS
1. *antibiotics*	—drugs used for bacterial infections (like pneumonia, strep throat, etc.)
2. *blood pressure*	—the pressure of the blood against the walls of the blood vessels (measured by two numbers, such as 120/80)
3. *fatigue*	—tiredness
4. *malpractice*	—bad treatment by a doctor, or other medical person
5. *prescribe*	—to order the use of a remedy
6. *prescription*	—order form for a remedy, usually signed by a doctor and brought to the drugstore
7. *psychiatric**	—referring to *psychiatry,* the science of treating mental or emotional illness

*Sh! Don't pronounce the *p* in *psychiatric* or *psychosomatic* or *psychology,* or any of the other words with *psych* in them.

8. *psychosomatic* —referring to physical problems caused by mental or emotional illness

9. *sick leave* —time off from work for sickness

10. *spa* —a hotel near springs of hot mineral water, where health treatments are given

11. *surgery* —medical treatment by operations (cutting open of the patient and removing the diseased part)

Nowadays, many people feel tired all the time. This chronic _____ makes it impossible for them to work. Some of them ask their bosses for _____ _____. They go to the doctor and say, "Please _____ something that will cure me." The doctor takes (measures) their _____ and does some other tests. If the doctor finds a bacterial infection, he (she) gives them a _____ for _____ and tells them to take it to the drugstore. Occasionally, the doctor finds that a person needs _____ to remove a diseased part. Sometimes the doctor finds nothing physically wrong and decides the problem may be _____. So he (she) asks the patient if he (she) wants to go to a _____ clinic. In Europe, doctors often send patients to a _____ to rest and bathe in the warm waters. But in North America, a doctor could be accused of _____ for doing this.

Now that you have learned these terms, see how they are used in a reading, and learn about cultural differences in medicine.

Is medicine international?

by Lynn Payer

While living in Europe and working there as a medical journalist, I was surprised by the differences between U.S. and European medicine. Why, for example, did the French talk about their livers all the time? Why did the Germans blame their hearts for their fatigue? Why did the British operate so much less than the Americans?

World travelers who have had to see a doctor in a foreign country have usually discovered that medicine is not quite an international science. The differences are so great that one country's treatment of choice may be considered malpractice across the border.

Some of the most commonly prescribed drugs in France are considered not effective in England and America. German doctors prescribe from six to seven times the amount of certain drugs for the heart as

doctors in France and England. But they prescribe fewer antibiotics. In the late 1960s American surgery rates were twice those of England. Since then this difference has become greater. Blood pressure considered high and requiring treatment in the United States might be considered normal in England. And the low blood pressure treated with 85 drugs as well as spa treatments in Germany is considered very healthy in the United States.

How can medicine, which is

A spa in France.

supposed to be a science, be so different in four countries? The answer is that culture has a great influence.

One example of this cultural influence is the prescription of sick leaves and trips to spas. French doctors place a great deal of emphasis on rest, sick leave, and spas. The French have the legal right to five weeks of vacation a year and no French man or woman would dream of not taking it. Some French people have refused high government appointments because they cause problems with their vacations. So, it is not surprising that French hospital stays are typically twice as long as those in the United States.

Long hospital stays, sick leaves, and "sleep cures" for psychiatric illness are favored in France. But it is considered even better to get out of the city and take the *cure* at a spa. One in every 200 medical visits in France results in a prescription for the *cure*. In 1984, over half a million persons took the *cure* with 95 percent of spa visits paid for at least in part by the health insurance. (In Germany the medical use of spas is even more common.)

The French pride themselves in their "specialized" spas. The spa doctor will write prescriptions for various treatments using the mineral waters and gases, prescribing the temperature and duration of treatment as well as what is to be done.

Spas, of course, are pooh-poohed in the United States and England. Their effect is considered psychosomatic. French spa doctors agree that some of the good effects of spa treatment are psychosomatic. But, they say, what is wrong with that? They do believe, however, that the good effects of spa treatments are more than psychosomatic.

One strong advocate of spas was the late Dr. Jacques Forestier, a doctor and scientist of international fame. Dr. Forestier was a trim and lively 82 when I interviewed him. Commenting on the British and North American disbelief in spas, he said: "It certainly shouldn't be said that they are behind us. It's simply a position they have taken. Medicine is not yet a very exact science, and there should still be room for many different points of view."

Medicine and Culture

TASK 1: TALKING IT OVER

1. What surprised the author when she lived in Europe?
2. How many weeks of vacation do all French people get? How does this compare with North American vacations? With vacations in your culture?
3. In your opinion is it good or bad to have a five-week vacation for everybody? Why?
4. What do you think a "sleep cure" is? In France, what kind of illness is it used for?
5. What do spa doctors prescribe for their patients? Would you like to go to a spa? Why or why not?
6. Who was Dr. Forestier? What did he think about spas? What did he think about North Americans who "pooh-poohed" the idea of spas?

TASK 2: CHARTING THE DIFFERENCES

Work with a partner. How many cultural differences in medicine can you find in the article? Fill out the following chart together, showing special features (aspects, characteristics) of medical practice in England, the United States, France, and Germany. One feature is already done for you. Report on your findings to the class and compare answers.

DIFFERENCES IN ATTITUDES TOWARD HEALTH AND MEDICINE

ENGLAND	U.S.	FRANCE	GERMANY
		people talk about their livers all the time	

TASK 3: SHARING IDEAS ABOUT HEALTH

Think of an object that you feel is related to health, either positively or negatively. It may be a bottle of aspirins, a piece of garlic, a cigarette, etc.). Put it (or a picture of it) in a box or a bag. Bring it to class. Sit in a circle with your classmates or a small group. Take turns telling about the objects and explaining why they are good or bad for health. Try to guess what each object is from the description; then show it.

THEME 2: COPING WITH SICKNESS

You wake up one morning and feel terrible. And this was the day you were planning to finish up a big project! Now all you want is to go back to sleep. What to do? First, think about what symptoms (signs of illness) you have. Then you will be better able to make a decision.

Study the vocabulary list below to learn ways of describing your symptoms.

A VOCABULARY OF SYMPTOMS AND SICKNESS

1. *cold, to have or catch a cold*   a common sickness in North America with some of these symptoms: sore throat, cough, runny (or stuffy) nose, and tiredness; colds are *contagious,* which means you catch them from others.

2. *constipation*		the common condition of not being able to go to the bathroom
3. *cough*		an irritation of the throat which causes a person to make a rasping sound
4. *diarrhea*		the common condition of having to go to the bathroom too often (opposite of constipation)
5. *fever*		a body temperature that is higher than normal (When fever goes up, you shiver and feel cold. When fever goes down, you sweat.)
6. *flu*		a very common sickness in North America, similar to a cold, but more severe and faster in its attack, often with a fever; *Flu* is contagious.
7. *headache, migraine*		pain in the head; a *migraine* is a very severe headache, often with pounding, sensitivity to light, and vomiting (throwing up the contents of the stomach)
8. *rash*		marks or spots on the skin, often red in color
9. *sore throat*		a painful feeling in your throat
10. *stomachache*		pains in your stomach

TASK 1: CHECKING COMPREHENSION

Tell whether each statement is true or false. Write *T* or *F* in the space provided. If it is false, correct it to make it true.

1. _____ A migraine is worse than just a simple headache.

2. _____ If you start feeling very cold, don't reach for the aspirins because your fever is going away.

3. _____ Red marks on the skin are called a *cough*.

4. _____ If you want to keep from catching a cold, don't go too near someone who has one.

5. _____ A flu is just a mild cold that doesn't cause much trouble.

6. _____ You should go to work when you have flu because this disease isn't contagious.

TASK 2: TALKING IT OVER

1. How do you get rid of (remove, eliminate) a headache? Do you take a remedy? Use massage or music or lie down in a dark room? Or do you just wait until it goes away? Explain.

2. If you have a cough, stomachache, diarrhea, or constipation, do you go to a drugstore and ask the advice of the pharmacist? Why or why not? Do you worry about the *side effects* of drugs?

3. When would you go to the doctor's office or clinic? To the Emergency Room of a hospital? What symptoms would you have?

4. Have you heard of *antibiotics?* In North America you can get them only with a doctor's prescription. Do you know when you should take antibiotics? And when you should *not* take them?

5. In your opinion, what is the best treatment for the common cold?

____ get lots of sleep

____ take vitamin C

____ do a lot of exercise

____ drink hot tea with honey and lemon

____ take two aspirins and a hot lemonade

____ drink lots of water and orange juice

____ eat chicken soup

____ Other?

6. Read the following joke about the common cold. Do you get the point?

An Old Joke About the Common Cold

PATIENT   Doctor, if I take these pills, how long will it take to get rid of my cold?

DOCTOR   With those pills it will take you about two weeks.

PATIENT   And without the pills?

DOCTOR   Without the pills, it will take about 14 days.

The Four Seasons

Spring   Summer   Fall   Cold and Flu

TASK 3: CALLING THE CLINIC—A DIALOGUE

Read the following dialogue aloud with a partner, twice. Take turns playing the role of Manuel. Then, if you have extra time, make up a dialogue with your partner about one of the situations below.

RECEPTIONIST	Good morning. Halverson Clinic. May I help you?
MANUEL	I would like to see a doctor.
RECEPTIONIST	Which doctor would you like to see?
MANUEL	I don't know. I've never been to the clinic before.
RECEPTIONIST	Do you have health insurance?
MANUEL	I think so. I have a student health card from the University.
RECEPTIONIST	That should do it. What seems to be your problem?
MANUEL	I'm tired all the time and I have a rash on my face.
RECEPTIONIST	Let me check the schedule. I have an opening with Dr. Schultz at 4:30 this afternoon. How's that?
MANUEL	That's fine. I'll be there. Could you please give me the address?
RECEPTIONIST	We are at 1724 E. Washington Avenue. It's right near campus.
MANUEL	Great. Thanks very much.
RECEPTIONIST	You're welcome. Goodbye.
MANUEL	Goodbye.

*IT WORKS!
Learning Strategy:
Role Playing
Improves Your
Social Skills*

Situation 1

You have a sore throat and a bad headache. You go to the drugstore and ask the pharmacist to advise you about remedies.

Situation 2

Your cousin comes to stay with you. It's 2 A.M. She wakes up with a cough and a very high fever, talking about seeing purple animals in the air. You call 911 (the emergency number) to ask for help.

TASK 4: OUTSIDE ASSIGNMENT: PREPARING FOR AN EMERGENCY

Look in the front pages of your phone book and find out what numbers you would call for different types of emergencies. In your opinion, what are the three most important numbers? Does your phone book give instructions for what to do in certain emergency situations? (Some phone books tell what to do in case of poisoning, robbery, earthquake, tornado, flood, etc., depending on the region.) Explain.

THEME 3: CHANGING CONCEPTS OF HEALTH AND ILLNESS

How does a healthy person look? Where does good health come from? Is it a gift from God or fate? Or do we cause our own good health? And is it our fault if we get sick? These are age-old questions, of course, and the answers to them are always changing. Let's take a look at some recent changes in the attitudes of North Americans about health.

A. Different Images of the Ideal Body Type

How much should a healthy person weigh? The answer to this question depends on many factors, including age, sex, and bone structure. It also depends on culture. In some cultures the ideal (perfect) body is thought to be heavy, and in others, thin. Even in the same culture the ideal is different during different time periods. In hard economic times, the perfect body is thought of as heavier, and in good economic times, it is thinner.

TASK 1: MAKING COMPARISONS

In North America, advertising has a great influence on the image of the ideal body type. In the last three decades, this image has gotten thinner and thinner. In the 1970s and 1980s it came to represent an impossible ideal, at least for most North Americans. In fact, it *was* impossible. Frequently, fashion photos are "trimmed" (cut with scissors) and then retaken. This means that even the models are not really as thin as they appear. Many people try to look like these false images. As a consequence, eating disorders like *anorexia* (the habit of eating very, very little) have become common, especially among girls and women.

The 1990s have brought some change of attitude, along with a new scale (chart of suggested weights). To find out about this new scale, look at the following selection from *Health* magazine.

In with the New Scale

by P.L. in *Health*

Barbara Bush and Delta Burke, Julia Child, and Oprah Winfrey.

These people may not be model-thin, but their weights are within the healthy range —according to a new table (see page 128). This new table was published in 1990 as part of the U.S. government's *Dietary Guide for Americans*. It approves a wider range of weights—both at the lower and upper limits—than does the Metropolitan Life table (the scale generally used in the past).*

---

*Like most weight charts in the U.S., this one uses pounds to measure weight. Canadian weight charts usually have measurement in both pounds and kilos. To convert pounds to kilos, divide the number of pounds by 2.205.

Height without shoes	Weight without clothes	
	Age 19 to 34*	35 and up*
5'0"	97–128	108–138
5'1"	101–132	111–143
5'2"	104–137	115–148
5'3"	107–141	119–152
5'4"	111–146	122–157
5'5"	114–150	126–162
5'6"	118–155	130–167
5'7"	121–160	134–172
5'8"	125–164	138–178
5'9"	129–169	142–183
5'10"	132–174	146–188
5'11"	136–179	151–194
6'0"	140–184	155–199
6'1"	144–189	159–205
6'2"	148–195	164–210
6'3"	152–200	168–216
Body Mass Index *Women or men	19–25	21–27

TASK 2: TALKING IT OVER

1. Do you think this scale would work in your culture? Why or why not?
2. Why do you think advertising is so important in North America? Is it also important in your culture? Explain.
3. In your opinion, why is dieting so popular among Americans and Canadians?
4. Which is harder: to lose weight or to gain weight? Why?

B. The Relationship Between Lifestyle and Illness

How does our behavior (the way we act) influence our health? What habits can make us more healthy? What habits can give us a higher risk of disease or death? The following selection from *Parade Magazine* presents common questions about the link between lifestyle and health, along with some answers from the author.

LEARNING STRATEGY

Forming Concepts: Guessing the meanings of words that you don't know from the context in which they occur helps you read more fluently.

GET READY TO READ:
GUESSING THE MEANING FROM CONTEXT

Before starting to read, learn some of the important words. Scan for each word by using the line number in parentheses. Look at the word's context. Then guess which of the synonyms or definitions is correct, and circle it. The words are given in order of their appearance.

1. disease **a.** pounding **b.** illness **c.** remedy

2. circulatory system **a.** system that breaks down food
   b. system that moves muscles and bones
   c. system that sends blood from the heart to the body

3. aerobics **a.** rapid continued exercises
   b. slow breathing techniques
   c. gentle massage treatments

4. fatal **a.** unkind **b.** embarrassing **c.** deadly

5. risky **a.** passive **b.** dangerous **c.** unusual

6. brisk **a.** active **b.** brief **c.** useful

7. excessive **a.** seasonal **b.** too much **c.** forbidden

Now read the selection to find out how to live longer.

Health: Take charge!
Questions you should ask

by Earl Ubell

QUESTION: *My habits weren't always healthy. Does this mean I will be sick when I'm old?*

ANSWER: It depends on how old you are now and how "unhealthy" your habits were. Research shows it's never too late to change and the time to start is now. In your 20s, 30s, and 40s, build a pattern of diet and exercise. It will protect you against diseases of the heart and circulatory system, which kill a million citizens a year.

A good, lifelong exercise pattern protects you against heart disease and other problems. Recommended is a three-way program of working with weights, flexibility training, and aerobics—exercise that sets your heart pounding and lungs inhaling oxygen quickly and deeply. Michael O'Shea, *Parade's* fitness expert, says a daily walking program is the easiest way to start. "At least 30 minutes of brisk walking every day will start your exercise schedule. It's safe and effective. You'll want to do more."

QUESTION: *Smoking, drinking, and fooling around? How bad can they really be?*

ANSWER: Pretty bad. (And we mean fatal, not naughty.) Evidence shows that cigarette smoking, taking more than two drinks a day and participating in risky behavior cause hundreds of thousands of deaths in the United States every year.

These risky behaviors figure highly in early deaths and severe injuries:

- Drinking and driving contributes to about 20,000 deaths a year.
- Smoking-related diseases—heart disease, lung and throat cancers, and emphysema (a serious lung complication)—took 434,000 lives in 1988 alone.
- Riding without wearing seat belts. Seat belts have saved 25,000 lives since 1983. You're three times more likely to need hospitalization without them.
- Unprotected sex (having sex without using a condom) can give you AIDS (and other diseases). Your risk is higher if you have many partners
- Excessive sunbathing can give you melanoma (a serious cancer of the skin).

So everything your mother told you not to do *is* risky. Mama was right!

Parade Magazine

TASK 1: WHAT'S YOUR ADVICE?

Read the following statements. Then give the necessary advice, based on the selection. The first one is done for you as an example.

1. You want to be free from AIDS.
   Advice: Unless you are in a safe relationship, don't have sex without protection. Go to the clinic or the drugstore and get some protection.
2. You want to live without lung cancer and throat cancer.
3. You want to be protected from heart disease.
4. You don't want to get melanoma of the skin.
5. You don't want to be put in the hospital after a car accident.
6. You don't want to be part of the statistic of "20,000 deaths a year."

TASK 2: TO AGREE OR NOT TO AGREE?

Work with two or three others. Take turns reading each opinion and decide if you agree or not. Talk about it until you reach a *unanimous decision* (one in which everyone agrees) about each one. (This may not be possible, but try.) Take notes and write down reasons for each decision. Your teacher may call on you to explain the opinions of your group.

a. A person has the right to do something risky—like excessive sunbathing—if he or she wants to. If it doesn't hurt anybody else, then it's nobody else's business.
b. It's silly to have a law about wearing seat belts.
c. Hospitals should have special, separate rooms where smokers can go and have a cigarette.

TASK 3: FACTS AND FALSEHOODS ABOUT AIDS

One of the biggest health concerns of our times is the fear of getting AIDS. How much do you know about this disease? Tell whether you think each of the following statements is true or false. Write *T* or *F* in the space provided. (Correct answers are in the Answer Appendix at the end of the book.)

1. _____ You can get AIDS by shaking hands with someone who has it.

2. _____ Many people catch AIDS from mosquito bites.

3. _____ It is not very likely that you'll get AIDS from a blood transfusion.

4. _____ Many drug addicts get AIDS because they use a needle from an infected person to inject themselves with a drug.

5. _____ It is impossible to get AIDS by having sex if a condom is used.

6. _____ All babies born to mothers with AIDS also get AIDS.

7. _____ AIDS can be transmitted by sneezing, coughing, or kissing.

8. _____ Everyone who gets AIDS dies within five years.

9. _____ There is no effective vaccine against AIDS.

10. _____ There are some drugs that can slow down the development of AIDS in HIV-positive* people.

TASK 4: DRAWING CONCLUSIONS FROM A CHART

How much exercise do North Americans get? How much of their leisure time (time when they have no work or obligations) is spent being active? The chart called *At Leisure: Americans' Use of Down Time* presents the results of a survey about this involving 6,000 Americans. Work alone or with a partner. Look at the chart and make some statements about Americans and exercise.

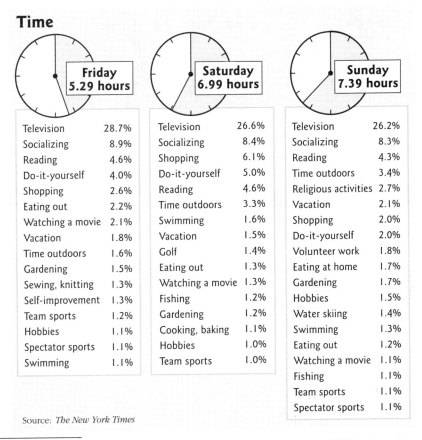

Time

Friday 5.29 hours		Saturday 6.99 hours		Sunday 7.39 hours	
Television	28.7%	Television	26.6%	Television	26.2%
Socializing	8.9%	Socializing	8.4%	Socializing	8.3%
Reading	4.6%	Shopping	6.1%	Reading	4.3%
Do-it-yourself	4.0%	Do-it-yourself	5.0%	Time outdoors	3.4%
Shopping	2.6%	Reading	4.6%	Religious activities	2.7%
Eating out	2.2%	Time outdoors	3.3%	Vacation	2.1%
Watching a movie	2.1%	Swimming	1.6%	Shopping	2.0%
Vacation	1.8%	Vacation	1.5%	Do-it-yourself	2.0%
Time outdoors	1.6%	Golf	1.4%	Volunteer work	1.8%
Gardening	1.5%	Eating out	1.3%	Eating at home	1.7%
Sewing, knitting	1.3%	Watching a movie	1.3%	Gardening	1.7%
Self-improvement	1.3%	Fishing	1.2%	Hobbies	1.5%
Team sports	1.2%	Gardening	1.2%	Water skiing	1.4%
Hobbies	1.1%	Cooking, baking	1.1%	Swimming	1.3%
Spectator sports	1.1%	Hobbies	1.0%	Eating out	1.2%
Swimming	1.1%	Team sports	1.0%	Watching a movie	1.1%
				Fishing	1.1%
				Team sports	1.1%
				Spectator sports	1.1%

Source: *The New York Times*

---

*HIV is the Human Immunodeficiency Virus—the virus that causes AIDS by invading and destroying helper T-cells of the body.

Keep a record in your journal of your activities for several days. (If you are artistic, illustrate it.) How much exercise do you get? Do you eat regular meals? Write a description of your lifestyle. Tell what parts you think are healthy and what parts unhealthy. Is your lifestyle similar to the typical North American lifestyle, or not? Has your lifestyle changed since you came to a new culture? If so, has it been for better or for worse?

THEME 4: THE INFLUENCE OF EMOTIONS ON HEALTH

Everyone knows that being sick can make you feel sad and depressed. But does it work the other way around? If you are feeling sad, can it make you sick? Can emotions influence your health?

A. Becoming Aware of Our Emotions

Many people are so busy that they never think about their emotions. "Me? Feel emotions?" they ask with surprise. But emotions (even if unknown) often show themselves in our bodies.

TASK 1: IDENTIFYING EMOTIONS

Look at the following list of emotions and make sure you understand their meaning. The emotions are listed in alphabetical order. Put them in order from the best, most positive emotion (1) to the worst or most negative (12). Compare with your classmates. Not everybody will have the same opinion about the order.

____	anger	____	happiness (joy)
____	boredom	____	irritation
____	contentment (satisfaction)	____	jealousy
____	excitement	____	resentment
____	fear	____	sadness
____	frustration	____	worry

TASK 2: WHAT WOULD YOU FEEL?

Write down the emotion(s) you would feel in each of the following situations. If you would feel no special emotion, write *N.E.* (no emotion). Compare with your classmates. Talk about why you answered as you did.

1. You meet an old friend after many years.
2. You are about to park your car when another car quickly takes the parking spot.
3. You are chosen to fly to Paris to represent your school in a contest.
4. Almost every day for a whole month your boss tells the same joke.
5. You arrive home and see a big package in plain brown paper.
6. You get the third highest mark in the class.
7. You are offered an interesting, high-paying job in a city far from your family.
8. A co-worker gets the promotion that you wanted.
9. It's midnight and someone knocks at the door.
10. Your cousin wins the lottery.

TASK 3: CAUSE AND EFFECT

Think of an emotional situation. Describe it in writing. On the back of the paper, write the name of the emotion you would feel in this situation. Read it to a group of three or four. Can they guess what emotion you wrote? Can you guess the emotions for their situations?

EXAMPLES: It's two o'clock in the morning and there is a lot of noise in the apartment under yours. (anger)

You win the lottery. (joy)

TASK 4: TALKING IT OVER

1. Which emotions give you a headache? A stomachache?
2. What other health problems can come from negative emotions?
3. Which emotions make you feel on top of the world?
4. Doctors say that even positive emotions can sometimes cause stress. Can you think of a situation to show this?
5. Do you think North Americans show their emotions? Which emotions?
6. Do people in your culture show their emotions in the same way?

LEARNING STRATEGY

Managing Your Learning: Taking time to relax and breathe deeply reduces stress and helps you learn better.

TASK 5: PRACTICING STRESS CONTROL

Do you understand the meaning of *stress*? Work with a partner and make a list of possible stressful situations. Compare lists with your classmates. Choose the three most stressful situations of all. Then, while someone reads them aloud, close your eyes and imagine you are experiencing them. Can you feel the stress? Try to relax and breathe deeply. Is there a difference? Could this really help someone or not? Are there better ways to control stress, such as music or exercise? Explain your opinion.

YOUR PERSONAL JOURNAL: PLOTTING YOUR UPS AND DOWNS

Do your moods change from day to day or stay the same? How do events in your life influence your emotions? Do they influence your health? Maybe you don't really know. Many people pay more attention to their work or to other people than to their own feelings. Here is your chance to find out more about yourself. First, draw a graph like the one in the illustration, with the weeks going across the top and descriptions on the side. (Change the graph to meet your needs.) Then go back to the *very beginning* of your journal. This is *Week 1*. Read your whole journal and use it to plot (make a visual record of) the ups and downs of your emotional condition. These guide questions can help you.

1. When was your emotional low point? Find the right week and make a dot there by *depressed* (or *out of sorts,* or whatever). Were there other low points? Fill those in too.
2. When was your emotional high point? Find the right week and make a dot by the correct description. Then fill in other high points.
3. How did you feel during the other weeks? Put a dot in the right place for all the weeks that are left.

When you finish, connect the dots. What kind of line do you have? Does it look like a mountain range? Or a highway? Try to explain your ups and downs. Do you know the reasons? What does your graph tell you about yourself?

B. A Native American View of Health

THEME 4:
THE INFLUENCE OF
EMOTIONS ON HEALTH

One of the divisions of conventional medicine is *psychiatry,* the practice of treating mental and emotional illness. Doctors who do this are called *psychiatrists.* Usually they use traditional ways, like talking about the patient's dreams and childhood experiences. But the following article from *Prevention* magazine tells about a psychiatrist who uses unusual methods. He uses methods based on the spiritual beliefs of the native people of North America.

GET READY TO READ:
GUESSING THE MEANING OF WORDS FROM CONTEXT

Scan the article for each of the following words. Use its form or context to guess which of the definitions is correct for it. (Test the definition by trying it in place of the word in the sentence.) The words are given in order of their appearance in the article.

WORDS	DEFINITIONS
1. _____ hike	**a.** bit of land next to the sea
2. _____ advise	**b.** task (especially in search of something)
3. _____ healing	**c.** give advice, recommend
4. _____ catch on	**d.** beginning of day, dawn
5. _____ clan	**e.** walk for a long way
6. _____ quest	**f.** understand
7. _____ seashore	**g.** curing, bringing (someone) to health
8. _____ daybreak	**h.** group of relatives

> **Threads**
>
> **Good thoughts are half of health.**
>
> Slavic proverb

The dance of healing

by Cathy Perlmutter

When patients tell their troubles to psychiatrist Carl Hammerschlag, M.D., he may suggest that they hike up a mountain. He may tell them to think about the flight of a young eagle. He might sing them a song from the Native American tradition or even advise that they perform a ritual with their family and friends.

"Some people think I'm a little crazy," laughs Dr. Hammerschlag, 50, who trained in psychiatry at Yale University. In fact, it was his 20 years spent practicing medicine in the American Southwest that changed his ideas about health and healing.

"Why people get sick, and why they get well, has to do with the connections between mind, body, and spirit," he says. "Native Americans have always known this. Western medicine is just beginning to catch on."

"In Western medicine, doctors tend to take most of the responsibility for making people well."

"Native American 'medicine men' understand that the healer plays but a small role in the healing process. They tell their patients, 'I'll

From "The Dance of Healing" by Cathy Perlmutter in PREVENTION, September 1989. Copyright © 1993 Rodale Press, Inc. All rights reserved.

do the best I can. You must do the best you can. You must have faith in yourself. You must ask for the support of your family and clan. We've all got to work together."

Quests for Health

As a psychiatrist, Dr. Hammerschlag works primarily in the area of emotional healing. "When a person is depressed or confused, the physician's advice is just one part of the prescription for spiritual renewal. The patient needs to learn to look within to find his or her own strength," says Dr. Hammerschlag. "It's like dancing. You can't learn to dance by listening to someone explain it to you; you have to get up and do it."

That's why Dr. Hammerschlag sometimes suggests that his patients undertake tasks or "quests," inspired by Native American traditions. He considers them useful lessons in what he calls the "dance of healing."

Create Your Own Tasks

Dr. Hammerschlag says you can create your own tasks according to what you need to learn:

"If you're sad and feeling down about the future, it won't make you feel better if someone tells you not to worry," Dr. Hammerschlag explains. "You've got to experience that sense of hopefulness for yourself. To do that," he says, "go to a beautiful place. There you will see

that from darkness comes the light. Camp out on a mountaintop, or walk along the seashore before daybreak."

"The idea is to experience the darkness and then the light of dawn."

"If you're fearful of a coming big move—changing jobs, buying a new home, going back to school—take a small, enjoyable risk. Ask yourself: 'What is it that I've always wanted to do? To learn to sail? To ski? To visit Alaska?' Pick one you'll enjoy and do it. Knowing you can succeed with the small risk will give you the strength to succeed with the bigger risk."

Prevention

TASK 1: CHECKING COMPREHENSION

1. A typical treatment of Dr. Hammerschlag is to advise his patient
   a. to take a strong drug
   b. to get an operation
   c. to listen to a song
2. He lived for 20 years
   a. in Alaska
   b. in the American Southwest
   c. at Yale University
3. He believes patients should ask for the help of
   a. the people they work with
   b. doctors and lawyers
   c. their families and clan
4. In his view a patient must look for strength
   a. in church
   b. in his work
   c. within himself
5. The doctor compares healing to
   a. a dance
   b. an eagle
   c. a mountain
6. To stop feeling sad about the future, you must
   a. think about how things are improving
   b. go to a beautiful place
   c. ask someone to tell you not to worry

TASK 2: TALKING IT OVER

1. In the Native American view, what connections are important to health?

2. Do you agree with Dr. Hammerschlag that Western medicine is "just beginning to catch on" to this idea? Explain.

3. In Western medicine, who takes responsibility for healing a person? And in Native American medicine? Which attitude seems more correct to you? Why?

4. What examples are there in the article of the *quests* or *tasks* people can do to feel better?

5. What quest or task would be good for someone who suffers from terrible dreams because of bad experiences in the past? For someone who is always worrying about work or studies (even when having success)?

6. Are psychiatrists popular in your culture? What do people with mental or emotional illness do to get help?

TASK 3: THE CIRCLE AND THE STONE

The Native Peigan and Cree Indians of Alberta, Canada have a custom at meetings. They sit in a circle and hand a stone from one person to another. The circle represents equality. There is no beginning and no end in a circle, no first or last place. The stone represents human nature. All stones are similar but each one is different and individual. An Elder holds the stone, says his or her name, and explains its meaning. The Elder then shares with the group something that he or she is thinking or feeling at that moment. Afterwards the stone is handed to the left. It's the next person's turn. This continues all around the circle.

Take a few minutes to think about what you want to say to your teacher and class. If possible, sit in a circle. Your teacher will take a stone (or some other object) and begin.

When it is your turn, say your name and where you are from. Tell something about yourself. You can tell about what you want to learn or do, about why you are happy or sad, about some event you are looking forward to, or about a friend or relative far away.

During this ceremony, you have the chance to express some ideas or feelings and to learn more about your teacher and classmates.

LOOKING BACK ON CHAPTER 6

Look at the goals on the first page of this chapter. How many did you accomplish? Are you working as hard now as you were at the beginning of this course? Review some key words from this chapter by doing the following vocabulary exercises. (Answers are given in the Answer Appendix at the end of the book.)

VOCABULARY REVIEW: FILLING IN THE RHYMING WORD

Complete the following jingles (short, rhyming phrases) with a rhyming key word from the chapter. The first letter of each word is there to help you. The first one is done as an example.

1. When you get a cold, you don't know what to do

    But it's even worse when you get the *f*_____*flu*_____.

2. Being in the mainstream is quite intentional

    If you use the medicine we call *c*_____.

3. Right to the clinic you'll want to dash

    If you look at your skin and see a *r*_____.

4. You certainly will feel a terrible pain

    If you get the headache we call a *m*_____.

5. In France a doctor might say to your Ma,

    Here's a prescription; now go to a *s*_____!

6. The doctors are brilliant. The doctors are old,

    But they still can't cure the common *c*_____.

7. Whatever is real

    Is never *i*_____.

8. Some people can feel a strong resentment

    One day, and the next: a true *c*_____

9. Native American doctors think that feeling

    is an important part of *h*_____.

138

VOCABULARY REVIEW: SYNONYMS

Match each word in the first column to its synonym(s) in the second column.

1. _____ chronic
2. _____ down
3. _____ excessive
4. _____ fatigue
5. _____ get rid of
6. _____ healing
7. _____ illness
8. _____ joy
9. _____ mainstream
10. _____ remedy
11. _____ risky
12. _____ surgery

a. cure
b. weight
c. operation
d. depressed
e. conventional
f. constant, continual
g. remove, eliminate
h. psychiatry
i. too much
j. happiness
k. sickness
l. medicine
m. tiredness
n. dangerous

Why Are Friendship and Love So Important?

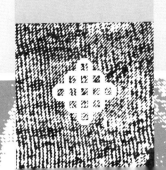

"A life without a friend is a life without a sun," according to an old German proverb. But who are our friends? Can we only love and form friendships with people similar to us? There are many different ideas about friendship, love, and marriage. New viewpoints on the roles of men and women, and on smaller groups in the dominant society, are emerging as North America changes, both its values (what it holds to be most important) and its words.

Think about some goals for your own improvement:

To learn more about:

- Different attitudes toward friendship and dating
- Different attitudes toward love and marriage
- Some recent changes in values and language in North America
- How to invite a friend to go out
- How to accept or decline an invitation

To practice skills:

- Participating in open discussions
- Analyzing stereotypes
- Writing a friendly letter
- Making *small talk* on safe topics
- Previewing and predicting for an extended reading
- Identifying the elements of a narrative

To acquire new vocabulary

THEME 1: FRIENDSHIP MEANS DIFFERENT THINGS TO DIFFERENT PEOPLE

Some have many friends and some have just a few. Some meet and talk with their friends almost every day. Others see them just once a month. There are friendships that end because one person moves away, and there are friendships that last across long distances and over many years until the end of life.

A. Who Is Your Friend?

Americans and Canadians have special relationships with people they consider their *good friends.* But they often use the simple word *friend* loosely. (That's why visitors sometimes get the false impression that North

Americans do not have deep friendships.) North Amercians call many people their friends—even people they've known a short time or people they see once in a blue moon (very rarely, not frequently). In fact, they sometimes refer to any person they *get along with* (do not fight with) as a friend.

TASK 1: USING THE WORD *FRIEND*

Which of the following people would you call a friend? Which one(s) do you think many North Americans would call a friend? (The answer to this is in the Answer Appendix at the end of the book.)

1. Someone you met about five years ago. The two of you get along well. You spend time together whenever you can. You talk a lot about different things: work, studies, hopes, and problems.
2. Someone you met about three months ago. You work in the same office, and once or twice a month you play badminton (or some other sport) together. You usually talk about work or activities.
3. Someone you know from childhood. You went to school together, but you rarely see each other. You send each other a card on birthdays or at Christmas. When you do see each other, you usually talk about the past.

TASK 2: A VOCABULARY OF RELATIONSHIPS

Here are some other words that describe the relationships between people. Which is which? (These answers are also in the Answer Appendix.)

a. acquaintances
b. classmates
c. co-workers
d. colleagues
e. neighbors

1. Mary and Kate live on the same block. They are both married and have children who play together.
2. Mary and Bruce often see each other at political meetings. They were introduced at a meeting about two months ago, and they usually talk for a few minutes before or after the meetings.
3. Bruce and Lang both work part-time at the same store. Sometimes they have the same work schedule.
4. Lang is taking an evening class at the university. In his class, he often talks to Kate, who is also taking the class.
5. Kate goes to school at night but during the day she runs a medical lab. Right now she is working closely with Barb (who works at a different lab) on an important new project.

TASK 3: THE BEST AND THE BRIEFEST

How do you briefly explain what a *good friend* is? Work in a group of three or four people to write five sentences that start with: *A true friend is someone who. . . .* Try to find the best ways of describing what you think a friend really is. Pool (put in all together) your ideas.* Finish the sentences in a positive or negative way. Here is an example of each. You may agree with them or you may not.

EXAMPLES: *A true friend is someone who laughs at your jokes.*

A true friend is someone who never asks you for money.

After you finish, compare definitions with other groups.

TASK 4: DESCRIBING OURSELVES AND OUR FRIENDS

What kind of people do you like to have for friends? Look at the following list of qualities (traits, characteristics) and choose the three most important ones for a friend. (Add other qualities to the list if you wish.) Compare with your classmates. Which qualities are the most popular?

adventurous	dependable	intelligent	serious
affectionate	easygoing	kind	sociable
aggressive	fun-loving	respectful	studious
athletic	honest	sensitive	thoughtful

TASK 5: GUESSING THE MEANINGS OF IDIOMS FROM MENTAL PICTURES

Now that you have learned a number of English idioms, you probably have a certain *feel* for them. Look at each word or phrase in the first column, and try to form your own picture of it in your mind. Then see if you can guess which of the people in the second column it would describe. (Answers are in the Answer Appendix.)

1. _____ a bookworm
2. _____ a doormat
3. _____ down to earth
4. _____ pig-headed
5. _____ pushy
6. _____ standoffish
7. _____ a tightwad
8. _____ uppity
9. _____ uptight
10. _____ warm-hearted

a. someone who won't listen to anyone else's ideas
b. a very nervous person
c. someone who is too careful with money
d. a continual reader who studies *all* the time
e. a kind and generous person
f. a snob who feels superior to everyone else
g. a person who is too aggressive
h. someone easily controlled by others
i. an unsociable person
j. a direct and practical person with no pretensions

*Suggestions for working together in group discussions are in the Preface.

TASK 6: DRAWING AND EXPLAINING

Draw your own illustration of one of the descriptive words or phrases from Task 5. Then explain why you would (or wouldn't) like to have a person with this quality for a friend.

B. Different Attitudes Toward Friendship

In Thailand, friends of the same sex often walk down the street, arm in arm, but friends of the opposite sex never touch each other in public. This is just the opposite of North American customs. Is your culture more like Thai culture or North American culture in this regard?

The following selection was written by an American who lived for many years in Thailand. Read the selection to learn more about the Thai idea of friendship.

GET READY TO READ:
SCANNING FOR WORDS

Scan the reading for the following. (They are given in the order of their appearance.)

1. A word that begins with *p* and means the opposite of *public:*

   _____.

2. A verb that begins with *s* and means "give something away":

   _____

3. Another way of saying *older:* _____

4. A synonym for *met:* _____.

5. A two-word phrase that means *without planning to:*

   _____.

6. A synonym for *similar* that starts with *a:* _____.

7. A synonym for *confused* that starts with *p:* _____.

Now read the selection to find out about a special way of viewing friendship.

"Die friends" and "eating friends"

by David C. Cooke

The Thais do not usually ask questions of a personal nature, though in some Asian countries this is considered not only quite proper but polite. The Thais feel, instead, that if anyone wishes to tell them anything about his private life, he will do so without being questioned. This sometimes strikes Westerners as a lack of interest, but to the Thais it is only proper courtesy.

One day I was out with Manoon Wongkomolshet and we met a friend of his. The two men talked for a few minutes before saying good-bye. When Manoon and I were alone again, he told me he had gone to school with the other man and had known him for many years.

I asked, "Does he have many children?"

"I don't know," Manoon replied. "He never told me, and I never asked."

Friendships play an important role in the life of the people. Among men, friends are often described as "die friends" or "eating friends." The "die friendship" is an ideal that is not often realized today, however, for it requires a willingness to sacrifice anything for the sake of the friend. Instead of using each others' names, men often refer to each other as *Pee* or *Nong*. *Pee* means Elder Brother, and *Nong* means Younger Brother.

There is also a similar friendship between girls.

One night at a party I was introduced to a young lady who had come in with another girl. The one I was talking with was named Kanjan, and I found out later that the other girl was named Soy.

As Kanjan and I talked, I asked her about Soy, and she said, "She is my sister. We came to Bangkok from the north, and we are living together here."

Several days later I encountered Kanjan again, by accident, in a store. She was alone, and I asked her about her sister.

"My sister is fine," she said. "But she could not come shopping with me. She had something else to do."

After a while I said, "You know, I would never have taken you two for sisters. You really don't look anything alike. I don't see any similarity at all."

"We don't have the same mother and father," Kanjan said. "That is the reason."

"But you said you are sisters," I replied, puzzled. "How can that be?"

"Because all Thai people consider all other Thai people to be their brothers and sisters," she said. "Soy and I would do anything for each other. We may not have had the same mother and father, but that does not matter. We are as close as true blood sisters could ever be."

Thailand, the Land of Smiles

TASK 1: TALKING IT OVER

1. How do Thais feel about personal questions? Why? Is this attitude typical of Asian people? Of North Americans?
2. Why didn't Manoon know if his good friend had children? What do you think of this?
3. What are the two types of friendship among Thais? What do you understand as the difference between the two? What different kinds of friendships do you have?
4. What do men who are good friends usually call each other?
5. Is Soy the sister of Kanjan or not? Explain.
6. In your culture, are some family words used for good friends? Explain.

TASK 2: THE TEST OF FRIENDSHIP

What would you sacrifice for a friend? Would you . . .

- lend him/her a large amount of money?
- drive him/her to work every day?
- take care of his/her children?
- give up your job for him/her?
- forgive him/her for doing something very mean to you?
- die for him/her?

Compare answers with your classmates.

TASK 3: THE MANY MEANINGS OF A SMILE

Thailand is often called "the land of smiles" because the people smile so much. Canadians and Americans smile a lot too, and like to think of themselves as friendly. A common way of showing friendliness is by smiling. Smiles in North America are usually associated with feeling happy. In other parts of the world, smiles can have different meanings. A smiling person may not feel happy at all.

Work with a partner. Look at the following. Which ones are possible in your culture? Which do you think are possible in other cultures? Explain.

A smiling person is someone who is ...

a. happy   e. angry   i. watched by others
b. nervous   f. obedient   j. traditional
c. respectful   g. frustrated   k. religious
d. friendly   h. dishonest   l. other? _____

TASK 4: HOW TO WRITE A FRIENDLY LETTER

If a plant is not watered, it will die. If friendship is not nurtured through special attentions, it can also die. One way to keep friendships alive over long distances and periods of time is to write letters. Look at the model for writing a friendly letter in English. Then answer the questions and do the assignment.

Name of City or Town
Date (Month, Day, Year)

Dear Joe (or Jill, etc.),

How are you? I hope you and your family are fine. (Then write a few lines asking about different family members or friends if you want to. Or go right into the next part: telling briefly how you and your family and mutual friends are doing.)

I want to tell you about . . . (Tell your friend something about your life, ideas, work, problems, or activities. Or if you like to share your private life, tell about your thoughts, emotions, and dreams.)

Well, it's time to bring this letter to a close. (Or you can say, I guess that's about all for now.) Hope to hear from you soon!

Love,*

Ann (or Mark, etc.)

P.S. My travel plans have been changed. I'm now going to . . . (and so on, with the message you almost forgot to include).

---

*Like the word *friend*, *Love* is often used loosely as a way to close letters (or to tell how much you *love* chocolate). It does not necessarily have a strong meaning. You may also use: *Fondly, With affection,* or the always acceptable *Yours truly,* but this last one is the least personal.

1. How do you open a friendly letter in your culture?
2. How do you close it?
3. Is there a way to add information at the end, like the English P.S. (which stands for *Post Script*)?
4. Do you like to get letters? Do you like to write them?
5. *Assignment:* Use the model letter for practice. Write a letter to a friend (or a relative you think of as a friend), following the model.

YOUR PERSONAL JOURNAL: A LETTER TO YOUR FORMER (PAST) SELF

Write a letter to yourself. Not to the self you are now. Look through your journal back to a time when you were in a different state of mind. (Maybe someone used a common English idiom to you that day and said, "You're not yourself today!") Give yourself a different name and write a letter, telling your opinions and feelings now about what that journal entry said.

TASK 5: WHAT DO YOU THINK OF "MAN'S BEST FRIEND"?

Man's best friend

Look at the photo of "man's best friend." Finish the statements with your opinions. Then compare statements with your classmates.

1. The reason many North Americans have *friendships* with pets is

   _____

2. In my culture, the attitude toward pets is (the same as in North America/somewhat similar/different/very different). Explain:

   _____

3. The animal I would prefer for a pet is a _____

   because _____

   _____

   _____

THEME 2: THE RITUALS OF SOCIALIZING AND DATING

Many unmarried Americans and Canadians join clubs or church groups in order to socialize. They want to make friends and meet people. Sometimes they have parties for the same reason. But the main social ritual is the date.

A date can mean going out with one other person or going out in a group.

TASK 1: WHAT IS A DATE?

Dating is a common custom in North America. Look at the photos and talk about dating customs in your culture.

TASK 2: CHOOSING SAFE TOPICS FOR STARTING CONVERSATIONS

According to an old saying, "Never discuss religion or politics over food because you are bound to have indigestion." Of course, many many people discuss both religion and politics at dinner, at lunch, or even at breakfast! They are two of the world's most interesting topics for dicussion.

In many parts of North America, however, these topics are not considered appropriate for conversations, especially not with strangers or people you don't know well. It's best to use small talk in such situations, polite conversation about safe topics that will not offend anyone. Think about this. Then write down four topics you consider would be good to use for small talk.

1. _____

2. _____

3. _____

4. _____

Compare with your classmates.

TASK 3: MAKING SMALL TALK

In pairs or groups of three, practice your skill with small talk. Pretend you are at a party or meeting with people you don't know well, and you

Threads

—Opposites attract.

—Love is blind.

English proverbs

must make conversation. Try to keep a conversation going for three to four minutes. Start with one of the "safe" topics. Change to a different one after a while, if necessary. Your teacher will tell you when to stop.

TASK 4: WHAT'S ACCEPTABLE?

Interview some Americans and/or Canadians about dating customs and fill in the chart with *yes* or *no* in each space. Fill out the other side for your culture. Then in small groups, or as a class, read each statement and compare the different answers. What conclusions or generalizations can you make about the different cultures and their attitudes toward dating? (Answers are given in the Answer Appendix.)

	U.S. OR CANADA	YOUR CULTURE
1. Dating starts in senior high school (grades 9–12)		
2. Dating starts in junior high school (grades 6–8)		
3. Young people usually go out in a group.		
4. Young people go out in couples.		
5. A girl may go out with a boy even if her parents do not know him.		
6. A girl can ask a boy to go out.		
7. The boy must ask a girl to go out.		
8. When a boy and a girl go out, each pays half ("going Dutch") or maybe just the girl pays.		
9. When a girl and a boy go out, the boy pays.		
10. If a boy and girl feel romantic, they *go steady* and do not date others.		

TASK 5: INVITING, ACCEPTING, AND DECLINING INVITATIONS

Work with a partner and make up phone conversations about the following. Take turns playing the different roles.

1. You call up a friend and invite him/her to go bowling. He/she declines because of too much work to do, but proposes another activity for tomorrow. You accept.
2. You call up someone you met at school and invite him/her to a party you and a friend are giving. He/she declines with an excuse.
3. Same as above, but he/she accepts. You give all the important details.

THEME 3: CHANGING VALUES, CHANGING LANGUAGE

There have been some big changes in North American society in the last 50 years. One change has been the appearance in the mainstream of groups that used to be excluded (left out).* Women, Hispanics, African-Americans, Asian-Americans, and people of other ethnic groups are now judges, doctors, lawyers, and engineers. Some hold important positions in government and industry. This was almost unheard of in the past. As a result, friendships and marriages in Canada and the United States today are no longer completely limited to the particular group into which a person is born. Are there groups that are excluded in your culture? Have there been changes?

A. Breaking Down Stereotypes

Prejudice and discrimination have existed over the years in many regions of North Amercia. Often certain groups have been used for negative stereotypes. A stereotype is an exaggeration or generalization which is falsely applied to a whole group. So, if *some* people from one group have green eyes, the stereotype shows them *all* with green eyes. If *some* of them are taking illegal drugs, the negative stereotype shows them *all* taking illegal drugs.

---

*This process has been only partly successful, but the change is evident.

TASK 1: IDENTIFYING STEREOTYPES

Identify which of the following are stereotypes and which are not. Why?

1. Many Scandinavians are tall.
2. Women are better than men at taking care of children.
3. Irish people eat lots of potatoes.
4. Latin Americans dance well.
5. A large number of the great violinists are Jewish.
6. African-Americans are good at sports.
7. Some men are aggressive.
8. Children are often afraid of the dark.
9. Americans are hard workers.

TASK 2: ANALYZING THE IDEA OF A STEREOTYPE

Not all stereotypes are negative. Some of them are positive. They present all the members of a certain group as having some good traits (qualities) or abilities. Are there some *positive stereotypes* in the exercise *Identifying Stereotypes?*

Now think about the following questions and write down your answers. When you finish, compare ideas with your classmates.

1. Most people agree that negative stereotypes are bad. What about positive stereotypes? Are they harmful too? Or are they all right? Explain.

   _____

   _____

   _____

2. Why do we make stereotypes, anyway? Is it because we fear the unknown?

   _____

   _____

   _____

TASK 3: COMMENTARY ON PHOTOGRAPHS

In the past, important jobs in North America were only held by white men. Now women and people of color (African-Americans, Native Americans, Mexicans, and others) hold some important positions. Other groups, like those with a different sexual orientation (men who date men and women who date women) were taboo in the past. Now they call themselves *gays* and *lesbians* and are gaining some political power. Look at the photos. Why would these photos surprise people from 50 years ago?

Left: Kim Campbell, the first woman to be Prime Minister of Canada. Right: Colin Powell, the first African-American to head the Joint Chiefs of Staff. Bottom: Gay AT&T employees delegation participate in the Gay and Lesbian Washington March.

YOUR PERSONAL JOURNAL: DESCRIBING "WE AND THEY"

Rudyard Kipling, a famous English poet from the beginning of this century, wrote a poem called *We and They.* One of the lines said, "All of the people like us are *we,* and everybody else is *they!*" This verse describes the thoughts of many in the world, especially people who have always lived in one place. Think back to when you were a child. How did you view your own culture? How did you view other cultures? Draw a line down the middle of one of your journal pages. Write *My Culture* on one side, and *Other Cultures* on the other. List all of the traits you associate with your own culture on the one side, and all those you associate with different cultures on the other. What negative and positive stereotypes are there?

B. New Words in the English Language

New people in power bring new ideas, new words. The English language is becoming more sensitive. Words are not supposed to project negative stereotypes. Government documents used to talk about *underdeveloped nations.* Now they talk about *developing nations.* The term for people with physical disabilities (those who can't walk or hear or see, for example) used to be *handicapped.* Now the term is *physically challenged.* The biggest change, however, is in words that refer to the roles of men and women. The following article focuses on one of these: *macho.*

"Macho" is a Spanish word that is often used in English. The original meaning in Spanish is *male* or *masculine.* But it has taken on a more negative meaning in English. Macho means having a strong and aggressive sense of male pride. Learn more about being (or not being) macho in the following article from the *Wall Street Journal.*

GET READY TO READ: UNDERSTANDING NUMERICAL COMPARISONS

The article uses several comparisons with numbers when it gives the results of a survey. Take time to understand them now so you can improve your reading of the article and of other articles. Match the written comparisons in the first column with the numerical figures in the second column.

1. _____ five times as many   **a.** 2/3

2. _____ two-thirds   **b.** 20%

3. _____ a little over one-third   **c.** 55%–60%

4. _____ one in five   **d.** 34%–35%

5. _____ two out of three   **e.** 5/1

6. _____ well over half   **f.** 66%

Men Claim Desire to Become Less Macho

by Alan L. Otten

Most men are looking for a warmer image, a new survey finds.

Nearly five times as many men would rather be seen as "sensitive and caring" than as "rugged and masculine." This is according to an in-depth survey of 1,000 men that was conducted by the Roper Organization.

The men were asked to choose words that best described themselves. About two-thirds checked off such terms as friendly, trustworthy, and kind. Only a little over one-third picked "athletic," and fewer than one in five saw themselves as "sexy." Adjectives such as affectionate and sociable were chosen much more often than expressions such as adventurous and aggressive.

Two out of three said men ought to be more caring and sensitive husbands and more caring and nurturing parents. Well over half thought it would be good if men were better able to show emotions in public—perhaps, for example, crying once in a while.

Many men, especially younger ones, are trying to move in these directions, Roper has found in previous surveys. "The 1990s will clearly be a time of transition for American men," says Roper's Thomas Miller.

Wall Street Journal

TASK 1: TALKING IT OVER

1. What are some of the words most men from the survey did not want as descriptions of themselves?
2. What words did they like better?
3. All right, men in the class: which would you prefer to be—athletic or kind? Sexy or trustworthy? Why?
4. Women in the class: would you rather marry an affectionate and sociable man, or an adventurous and aggressive one? Why?
5. In your opinion, should men be more caring and nurturing? Should they cry in public? Why or why not?
6. How do you explain the changes in the North American image of manliness? Are there changes in your culture too? Explain.
7. Nowadays, the term *police officer* is generally used instead of *policeman*. Are there any new words like this in your native language?

TASK 2: WHAT ARE THE NEW WORDS?

Can you match old terms to the new ones?

OLD TERMS	NEW TERMS
1. _____ fireman	**a.** letter carrier
2. _____ chairman	**b.** milk carrier
3. _____ mailman	**c.** fire fighter
4. _____ milkman	**d.** chair

Calvin and Hobbes   **Bill Watterson**

THEME 4: LOVE AND/OR MARRIAGE

Everybody knows that the roles of men and women are changing, and not just in North America, but all over the world. Still, the force of tradition is strong, and people delight in old customs.

A. Weddings And Marriages

There are many types of weddings, and many views of love and marriage. These questions are of great importance to the structure of society, but at the same time they are intensely personal and private. Sometimes this causes conflicts.

A traditional wedding in North America takes place in a church (or temple or mosque), but many other ways of celebrating a marriage are also popular. Formal clothing for the bride and groom, bridesmaids and groomsmen is common, but today this can be very expensive. A wedding can easily cost $15,000. So, many couples choose less formal (and less expensive) alternatives. Some simply get married by a Justice of the Peace (a government official), especially if it is a second or third (or more) marriage. Some elope (run off and get married without telling anyone in advance).

TASK 1: TALKING IT OVER

1. What do you think of the wedding in the photo? Why?
2. Have you been to a wedding in North America? What was it like?
3. The following traditions are common at North American weddings. Can you guess the symbolism of each? Do these or similar traditions exist in your culture?
   a. The father or another older relative of the bride "gives the bride away" to the groom.
   b. During the ceremony, the bride and groom exchange rings. The wedding rings are worn on the left hand.
   c. The bride and groom kiss after they are pronounced "husband and wife."
   d. As the bride and groom walk out, people throw rice over them.
   e. The bride and the groom cut the wedding cake together and then feed some to each other.
4. What is a traditional wedding like in your culture? Are there other alternatives today? Do couples sometimes elope?

Threads

The torch of love is lit in the kitchen.

French proverb

TASK 2: A GROUP DISCUSSION ON THE ROLES OF MEN AND WOMEN

Every culture has its beliefs and "rules" about the roles of men and women. Of course, you may have the same beliefs as the general beliefs in your culture, or you may have different ones. Use the survey below to help you explore your opinions about the roles of men and women. Try to answer quickly, giving your first reaction to each statement. After you answer, compare your response to what you think is common in your culture.

For this activity, you may want to separate into two groups, all males and all females. Or you may want to separate into groups of married people and single people. Choose one member to take down the opinions of the group, and another member to write down comments people make. At the end of the discussion, a different member of each group should give the results of the survey. Be sure to tell about any comments that are particularly interesting.

	AGREE	DISAGREE	NO OPINION	COMMENTS
1. People should not marry before 21.				
2. Men should be responsible for the main income of the family.				
3. Women with young children should not work.				
4. Both men and women should do housework and cooking.				
5. Men should cook several times a week.				
6. It's best to wait several years after marriage to have children.				
7. The ideal family has two children.				
8. There is nothing wrong with a couple who decide not to have children.				

	AGREE	DISAGREE	NO OPINION	COMMENTS
9. There is nothing wrong with a person who decides not to marry at all.				
10. Boys and girls should live with their parents until they marry.				

TASK 3: OUTSIDE ASSIGNMENT: CONDUCTING A SURVEY

Give the survey to three or more Americans or Canadians. Be sure to write down whether the person is male or female and married or single. Then bring these results to class. Compare the responses to those from your own classmates. Are they similar? Are they different? Where do you find most of the differences?

B. An Extended Reading Challenge: *Chinua Achebe's Marriage Is a Private Affair*

This is not a small challenge. The following story is by a famous writer, Chinua Achebe. It is about the conflict between love and family. Achebe's novels and stories are read in all parts of the English-speaking world and have also been translated into many languages. His writing forms part of the course of studies at many North American universities. This is an example of changing values because Chinua Achebe is from Nigeria. Years ago, almost no books from Africa were included in the North American university curriculum. The following story is long and is presented here in its original form, without abbreviation or adaptation. You should use it to practice techniques for extended (longer) readings.

GET READY TO READ: PREVIEWING AN EXTENDED READING

This is a longer English reading than any you have had in this book up until now—at least four times as long. Before beginning to read something long, take a couple of minutes to look over the whole thing (except for the end since you don't want to read the ending of the story). Use the title, illustrations, and divisions to try to guess a bit of what the story is about.

1. Write a short statement about that here:

_____

_____

_____

Compare your statement with those of your classmates.

2. The story is divided into four parts to make it easier for you. There is some help before and after each one. How long do you think it will take you to read each part? _____ Check your time when you read and see if you were right.

3. Read each part of the story at least twice. Don't look up any words in the dictionary the first time. Skip over them and see if you can understand them the second time around. Make a list of words that really bother you and then ask your teacher or classmates for help.

GET READY TO READ: IDENTIFYING THE NARRATIVE ELEMENTS AND PREDICTING THE ACTION OF PART 1

The three main elements of any story are the *setting* (a general idea of where and when it takes place), the *characters,* and the *plot* (the action). The first two are usually identified early. Take about two minutes to scan Part 1 for them. Then, help yourself get started by identifying them here:

1. Setting: Time   _____   Place _____
2. Main Characters: _____ ,   and _____ .

You know that if everything is fine, there is no story. So you can guess that there will soon be a problem of some type. Make a prediction about the plot by finishing this statement:

Prediction: These two people who are so much in love will soon have a problem with

_____

_____

_____

_____

Marriage Is a Private Affair

by Chinua Achebe

Part 1: Two People In Love*

"Have you written to your dad yet?" asked Nene one afternoon as she sat with Nnaemeka in her room at 16 Kasanga Street, Lagos.

"No. I've been thinking about it. I think it's better to tell him when I get home on leave!"

"But why? Your leave is such a long way off yet—six whole weeks. He should be let into our happiness now."

Nnaemeka was silent for a while, and then he began very slowly as if he groped for his words: "I wish I were sure it would be happiness to him."

"Of course it must," replied Nene, a little surprised. "Why shouldn't it?"

"You have lived in Lagos all your life, and you know very little about people in remote parts of the country."

"That's what you always say. But I don't believe anybody will be so unlike other people that they will be unhappy when their sons are engaged to marry."

"Yes. They are most unhappy if the engagement is not arranged by them. In our case it's worse—you are not even an Ibo."

This was said so seriously and so bluntly that Nene could not find speech immediately. In the cosmopolitan atmosphere of the city it had always seemed to her something of a joke that a person's tribe could determine whom he married.

At last she said, "You don't really mean that he will object to your marrying me simply on that account? I had always thought you Ibos were kindly-disposed to other people."

"So we are. But when it comes to marriage, well, it's not quite so simple. And this," he added, "is not peculiar to the Ibos. If your father were alive and lived in the heart of Ibibio-land he would be exactly like my father."

"I don't know. But anyway, as your father is so fond of you, I'm sure he will forgive you soon enough. Come on then, be a good boy and send him a nice lovely letter. . . ."

"It would not be wise to break the news to him by writing. A letter will bring it upon him with a shock. I'm quite sure about that."

"All right, honey, suit yourself. You know your father."

As Nnaemeka walked home that evening he turned over in his mind different ways of overcoming his father's opposition, especially now that he had gone and found a girl for him. He had thought of showing his letter to Nene but decided on second thoughts not to, at least for the moment. He read it again when he got home and couldn't help smiling to himself. He remembered Ugoye quite well, an Amazon of a girl who used to beat up all the boys, himself included, on the way to the stream, a complete dunce at school.

"I have found a girl who will suit you admirably—Ugoye Nwke, the eldest daughter of our neighbor Jacob Nwke. She has a proper Christian upbringing. When she stopped schooling some years ago her father (a man of sound judgement) sent her to live in the house of a pastor where she has received all the training a wife could need. Her Sunday School teacher has told me that she reads her Bible very fluently. I hope we shall begin negotiations when you come home in December.

---

*The divisions are not in the original story but are included for teaching purposes.

TASK 1: TALKING IT OVER

1. How are Nene and Nnaemeka different?
2. How are they similar?
3. What difference of opinion do they have about Nnaemeka's father?
4. In your opinion, why didn't Nnaemeka show the letter to Nene? Do you think he should have?
5. Who is Ugoye, and what is she like?

TASK 2: DISCUSSION

Is it wrong to disobey your father?

GET READY TO READ: PREDICTING THE ACTION OF PART 2

Think about what you know (indirectly, of course) about Nnaemeka's father. Skim the next part for one minute, and then finish the following prediction:

Prediction: The reaction of Nnaemeka's father will be

_____

_____

_____

Read to see if you are right.

Part 2: A Conversation with Father

On the second evening of his return from Lagos, Nnaemeka sat with his father under a cassia tree. This was the old man's retreat where he went to read his Bible when the parching December sun had set and a fresh, reviving wind blew on the leaves.

"Father," began Nnaemeka suddenly, "I have come to ask for forgiveness."

"Forgiveness? For what, my son?" he asked in amazement.

"It's about this marriage question."

"Which marriage question?"

"I can't—we must—I mean it is impossible for me to marry Nweke's daughter."

"Impossible? Why?" asked his father,

"I don't love her."

"Nobody said you did. Why should you?" he asked.

"Marriage today is different . . ."

"Look here, my son," interrupted his father, "nothing is different. What one looks for in a wife are a good character and a Christian background."

Nnaemeka saw there was no hope along the present line of argument.

"Moreover," he said, "I am engaged to marry another girl who has all of Ugoye's good qualities, and who . . ."

His father did not believe his ears. "What did you say?" he asked slowly and disconcertingly.

"She is a good Christian," his son went on, "and a teacher in a Girls' School in Lagos."

"Teacher, did you say? If you consider that a qualification for a good wife I should like to point out to you, Nnaemeka, that no Christian woman should teach. St Paul in his letter to the Corinthians says that women should keep silence." He rose slowly from his seat and paced forwards and backwards. This was his pet subject, and he condemned vehemently those church leaders who encouraged women to teach in their schools. After he had spent his emotion on a long homily he at least came back to his son's engagement, in a seemingly milder tone.

"Whose daughter is she, anyway?"

"She is Nene Atang."

"What!" All the mildness was gone again. "Did you say Neneataga? What does that mean?"

"Nene Atang from Calabar. She is the only girl I can marry." This was a very rash reply and Nnaemeka expected the storm to burst. But it did not. His father merely walked away into his room. This was most unexpected and perplexed Nnaemeka. His father's silence was infinitely more menacing than a flood of threatening speech. That night the old man did not eat.

When he sent for Nnaemeka a day later he applied all possible ways of dissuasion. But the young man's heart was hardened, and his father eventually gave him up as lost.

"I owe it to you, my son, as a duty to show you what is right and what is wrong. Whoever put this idea into your head might as well have cut your throat. It is Satan's work." He waved his son away.

"You will change your mind, Father, when you know Nene."

"I shall never see her," was the reply. From that night the father scarcely spoke to his son. He did not, however, cease hoping that he would realize how serious was the danger he was heading for. Day and night he put him in his prayers.

TASK 3: TALKING IT OVER

1. What does Nnaemeka's father think about the need for love in marriage? What does Nnaemeka think? What do you think?
2. What does Nnaemeka's father think are the qualities of a good wife? And you?
3. What kind of man is the father? Why do you think his son is different from him?
4. How does the father surprise his son?

TASK 4: DISCUSSION

Is similarity of background desirable in someone you wish to marry? Why or why not?

GET READY TO READ:
PREDICTING THE ACTION OF PART 3

You have met Nnaemeka's father and now you will meet other men of the Ibo culture. What do you think they will say about Nnaemeka's marriage? Make a prediction:

Prediction: The reaction of the Ibo men will be

_____

_____

_____

Part 3: Men of the Ibo Culture Talk Together

Nnaemeka, for his own part, was very deeply affected by his father's grief. But he kept hoping that it would pass away. If it had occurred to him that never in the history of his people had a man married a woman who spoke a different tongue, he might have been less optimistic. "It has never been heard," was the verdict of an old man speaking a few weeks later. In that short sentence he spoke for all of his people. This man had come with others to commiserate with Okeke when news went round about his son's behaviour. By that time the son had gone back to Lagos.

"It has never been heard," said the old man again with a sad shake of his head.

"What did Our Lord say?" asked another gentleman. "Sons shall rise against their Fathers; it is there in the Holy Book."

"It is the beginning of the end," said another.

The discussion thus tending to become theological, Madubogwu, a highly practical man, brought it down once more to the ordinary level.

"Have you thought of consulting a native doctor about your son?" he asked Nnaemeka's father.

"He isn't sick," was the reply.

"What is he then? The boy's mind is diseased and only a good herbalist can bring him back to his right senses. The medicine he requires is *Amalile,* the same that women apply with success to recapture their husband's straying affection."

"Madubogwu is right," said another gentleman. "This thing calls for medicine."

"I shall not call in a native doctor." Nnaemeka's father was known to be obstinately ahead of his more superstitious neighbours in these matters. "I will not be another Mrs. Ochuba. If my son wants to kill himself let him do it with his own hand. It is not for me to help him."

"But it was her fault," said Madubogwu. "She ought to have gone to an honest herbalist. She was a clever woman, nevertheless."

"She was a wicked murderess," said Jonathan who rarely argued with his neighbours because, he often said, they were incapable of reasoning. "The medicine was prepared for her husband, it was his name they called in its preparation and I am sure it would have been perfectly beneficial to him. It was wicked to put it into the herbalist's food, and say you were only trying it out."

Six months later, Nnaemeka was showing his young wife a short letter from his father:

Threads

A lovesick person looks in vain for a doctor.

West African proverb

"It amazes me that you could be so unfeeling as to send me your wedding picture. I would have sent it back. But on further thought I decided just to cut off your wife and send it back to you because I have nothing to do with her. How I wish that I had nothing to do with you either."

When Nene read through this letter and looked at the mutilated picture her eyes filled with tears, and she began to sob.

"Don't cry, my darling," said her husband. "He is essentially good-natured and will one day look more kindly on our marriage." But years passed and that one day did not come.

TASK 5: TALKING IT OVER

1. What was the main argument of the Ibo men against the marriage of Nnaemeka and Nene?
2. Are the Ibo men Christian, or do they practice native African religion?
3. You have to "read between the lines" to understand the story of Mrs. Ochuba. Who was she, and what did she do wrong?
4. What letter did Nnaemeka show to Nene? What did it contain? What emotions do you think Nene felt when she saw it?

TASK 6: DISCUSSION

An old saying in English goes like this: *You only hurt the ones you love.* Is this true? In the story, who is hurting whom? Why?

Now you are near the end of the story. Do you think the author will make it happy or sad?

Prediction: I think the ending of this story will be

_____

_____

_____

Part 4: Actions and Reactions

For eight years, Okeke would have nothing to do with his son, Nnaemeka. Only three times (when Nnaemeka asked to come home and spend his leave) did he write to him.

"I can't have you in my house," he replied on one occasion. "It can be of no interest to me where or how you spend your leave—or your life, for that matter."

The prejudice against Nnaemeka's marriage was not confined to his little village. In Lagos, especially among his people who worked there, it showed itself in a different way. Their women, when they met at their village meeting, were not hostile to Nene. Rather, they paid her such excessive deference as to make her feel she was not one of them. But as time went on, Nene gradually broke through some of this prejudice and even began to make friends among them. Slowly and grudgingly they began to admit that she kept her home much better than most of them.

The story eventually got to the little village in the heart of the Ibo country that Nnaemeka and his young wife were a most happy couple. But his father was one of the few people in the village who knew nothing about this. He always displayed so much temper whenever his son's name was mentioned that everyone avoided it in his presence. By a tremendous effort of will he had succeeded in pushing his son to the back of his mind. The strain had nearly killed him but he had persevered, and won.

Then one day he received a letter from Nene, and in spite of himself he began to glance through it perfunctorily until all of a sudden the expression on his face changed and he began to read more carefully.

"Our two sons, from the day they learnt that they have a grandfather, have insisted on being taken to him. I find it impossible to tell them that you will not see them. I implore you to allow Nnaemeka to bring them home for a short time during his leave next month. I shall remain here in Lagos . . ."

Threads

The heart that loves is always young.

Greek proverb

The old man at once felt the resolution he had built up over so many years falling in. He was telling himself that he must not give in. He tried to steel his heart against all emotional appeals. It was a re-enactment of that other struggle. He leaned against a window and looked out. The sky was overcast with heavy black clouds and a high wind began to blow filling the air with dust and dry leaves. It was one of those rare occasions when even Nature takes a hand in a human fight. Very soon it began to rain, the first rain in the year. It came down in large sharp drops and was accompanied by the lightning and thunder which mark a change of season. Okeke was trying hard not to think of his two grandsons. But he knew he was now

fighting a losing battle. He tried to hum a favourite hymn but the pattering of large rain drops on the roof broke up the tune. His mind immediately returned to the children. How could he shut his door against them? By a curious mental process he imagined them standing, sad and forsaken, under the harsh angry weather—shut out from his house.

That night he hardly slept, from remorse—and a vague fear that he might die without making it up to them.

TASK 7: TALKING IT OVER

1. How many years went by with no change of heart from Nnaemeka's father? Have you ever heard of long silences among members of the same family? What reasons are there?
2. How did the women show their prejudice against Nene? What did she do?
3. Why didn't Nnaemeka's father hear about the good traits of the young couple?
4. What happened to change the father's heart?
5. In your opinion, is the ending a happy one?

TASK 8: DISCUSSION

Do you think there are really people like Nnaemeka's father? Is the story realistic or not? Explain.

TASK 9: ONE DAY LATER

Work alone or in a group. Write the letter that Nnaemeka's father sends to his son, or present a short scene to show what happens the day after the end of this story. Make it Part 5 and give it a title.

Look at the first page of this chapter. Did you fulfill most of your goals, at least in part? Are you reading books or magazines or newspapers now, or at least parts of them? Are you watching TV or listening to the radio? Are you writing letters in English, and making small talk every chance you get? Take a moment to review key words from this chapter by doing the exercises that follow. (Answers are given in the Answer Appendix.)

VOCABULARY REVIEW: ANTONYMS

Match each word from the first column with an antonym from the second column.

1. _____ acquaintance		**a.** public
2. _____ adventurous		**b.** masculine
3. _____ easygoing		**c.** sociable
4. _____ exclude		**d.** stranger
5. _____ get along		**e.** generous
6. _____ macho		**f.** include
7. _____ private		**g.** fearful
8. _____ tightwad		**h.** uptight
9. _____ standoffish		**i.** elope
		j. fight
		k. sensitive

VOCABULARY REVIEW: SYNONYMS

Match each word in the first column to its synonym, or short definition, in the second column.

1. _____ aggressive		**a.** false generalization
2. _____ colleague		**b.** postscript
3. _____ dating		**c.** quality
4. _____ encounter		**d.** action
5. _____ mailman		**e.** worker in the same profession
6. _____ P.S.		**f.** polite conversation
7. _____ pet		**g.** survey
8. _____ plot		**h.** pushy
9. _____ setting		**i.** going out together
10. _____ small talk		**j.** marriage
11. _____ stereotype		**k.** animal friend
12. _____ trait		**l.** letter carrier
		m. time and place
		n. find

168

Now that you have finished the last chapter, think about what you have learned during the whole course. Prepare the following general review. Share and compare answers with your class.

1. DIFFERENCES AND SIMILARITIES

Write down some differences between North American culture and your culture (or a different culture). Then write down some similarites between them. Use themes from the following list as a guide, or add others if you wish.

1. Classroom interactions
2. Introducing yourself
3. Making conversation
4. Meal schedules
5. Buying foods
6. Eating and drinking
7. Expressing emotions
8. Measuring time with calendars
9. Prejudice and discrimination
10. Using doctors and medicine
11. Making friends
12. New words and attitudes
13. Getting married
14. Speaking about your opinions

2. GIVING ADVICE TO A NEWCOMER

Imagine that you are going to talk with a friend from your culture who will be coming to North America for the first time. What advice would you give to him or her about some of the above themes?

3. EXPLAINING WITH EXAMPLES

Give examples to support three of the following statements:

1. Learning idioms can help you to communicate better in English.
2. Charts and graphs are useful ways to categorize and understand information.
3. Developing certain skills can help you to read better.
4. We often communicate without words.
5. By observing people, we make surprising discoveries about habits and customs.

4. ANSWERING A QUESTION FROM ONE OF THE TITLES

The titles of chapters 2 through 7 are questions. Choose one of them and write a good answer to it in the form of a paragraph.

Appendix

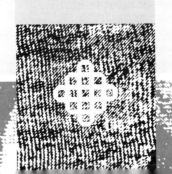

CHAPTER 1

Guessing and Drawing Conclusions, page 4. 1. All three photos were taken in North America, two in the United States and one in Canada. Left photo: San Francisco's Chinatown; top, Ukrainian festival, Dauphin, Manitoba; bottom, Feast of the Blessed Mother, North End, Boston.

Guessing the Mystery Words, page 9. 1. touch 2. sight 3. taste 4. hearing 5. smell

Playing with Optical Illusions, pages 18-19. 1. Both lines are exactly the same length. Take out your ruler and measure them. 2. The picture shows an impossible construction. Several different steps could be the top or bottom step. It depends on how you look at it. 3. All the lines are perfectly straight. The wavy horizontal lines make them APPEAR wavy too.

CHAPTER 2

Similarities Among Greeting Styles: A General View, page 26. In all five cases, the first answer (a) is the usual, expected answer.

Three Idioms, page 36. 1. to do something to take away the shyness from a group of people and make them feel more comfortable. 2. to find subjects everybody agrees upon and people all have the same ideas about. 3. (to) understand.

Vocabulary Review: Synonyms (Looking Back on Chapter 2), page 40. 1. d 2. i 3. g 4. j 5. h 6. b 7. a 8. c. 9. f **Vocabulary Review: Antonyms,** page 40. 1. uncomfortable 2. respectful 3. upward 4. gentle 5. informal, casual 6. unfriendly 7. goodbye 8. rude 9. courtesy, politeness 10. difference

CHAPTER 3

Learning New Idioms, page 45. 1. to start (or continue) some work or activity and not let it stop. 2. to get very upset about some little thing that is not important. 3. to hear something and understand that it is probably not completely true.

Vocabulary Review: Synonyms and Short Definitions (Looking Back on Chapter 3), page 61. 1. m 2. g 3. l 4. f 5. n 6. j 7. d 8. c 9. k 10. e 11. a 12. i **Vocabulary Review Word Families,** page 61. 2. explaining, explanation 3. introduce, introducing 4. describe, describing 5. pronouncing, pronunciation 6. inform, information 7. assign, assigning 8. suggest, suggestion 9. agree, agreeing

CHAPTER 4

Crossword Puzzle (Looking Back on Chapter 4), page 90. *Across:* 3. taboo 4. pork 5. vegetarian 7. schedule 9. brunch 10. ethnic 11. diversity 14. relative 15. lettuce 16. coupons 19. elbows 20. grapes; *Down:* 1. embarrassing 2. staples 6. ate 8. utensils 11. delicacy 12. ritual 13. taco 17. origin 18. please. Mystery Word: Yum!

CHAPTER 5

Vocabulary Review: Scrambled Letters, (Looking Back on Chapter 5), page 113. 1. New Year Resolutions 2. hangover 3. lunar calendar 4. prejudice 5. leap year 6. valentine day 7. patriotic 8. to pull your leg **Vocabulary Review: Word Families,** page 114. 2. categorize, categorizing 3. predicting, prediction 4. legislate, legislating 5. celebrating, celebration 6. create, creation 7. decorate, decorating 8. discriminate, discrimination 9. appreciating, appreciation

CHAPTER 6

Facts and Falsehoods about AIDS, pages 130–131. 1. False. This could happen only if both people had huge, bleeding wounds on their hands. 2. False. Not one case of AIDS from a mosquito bite has ever been proved, and the subject has been widely examined. 3. True. Nowadays in North America there is only a very very small risk of getting AIDS from a blood transfusion because the blood is tested effectively. 4. True. This is one of the two common ways of getting AIDS. (The other is from unprotected sex.) 5. False. If the condom is not used carefully or has a hole in it, a person using it can still get AIDS. But the use of a condom during sex greatly reduces the possibility of getting AIDS. 6. False. Only about 40% of babies born to mothers with AIDS get the disease. 7. False. AIDS is not transmitted through the air; it is transmitted through blood or semen. 8. False. Many victims of AIDS die within five years, but some have lived much longer than that. 9. True. As of 1993, there is no effective vaccine against AIDS on the market. However, scientists think they are very close to developing one. 10. True. There are some drugs that can slow down AIDS now, and scientists are working on producing many new ones.

Vocabulary Review: Filling in the Rhyming Word (Looking Back on Chapter 6), page 138. 2. conventional 3. rash 4. migraine 5. spa 6. cold 7. ideal 8. contentment 9. healing **Vocabulary Review: Synonyms,** page 139. 1. f 2. d 3. i 4. m 5. g 6. a 7. k 8. j 9. e 10. l 11. n 12. c

CHAPTER 7

Using the Word *Friend*, page 143. Most North Americans would refer to all three of these people as *friends*. Only the first one (#1), however, would be called a *good friend* or *best friend*.

A Vocabulary of Relationships, page 143. 1. e 2. a 3. c 4. b 5. d

Guessing the Meanings of Idioms from Mental Pictures, page 144. 1. d 2. h 3. j 4. a 5. g 6. i 7. c 8. f 9. b 10. e

Different Attitudes Toward Friendship, page 145. You would almost never see a scene like this in the United States or Canada because the two girls are holding hands. In North America, adults (or even older children) of the same sex do not hold hands, especially not in public. It would make most Americans or Canadians very uncomfortable for someone of the same sex to take their hand, while walking down the street.

What's Acceptable? page 150. All ten statements show acceptable ways of dating in North America. Individual families have their own guidelines, as do religions. Some are strict and some are not.

Vocabulary Review: Antonyms (Looking Back on Chapter 7), page 168. 1. d 2. g 3. h 4. f 5. j 6. k 7. a 8. e 9. c **Vocabulary Review: Synonyms** 1. h 2. e 3. i 4. n 5. l 6. b 7. k 8. d 9. m 10. f 11. a 12. c